I0488962

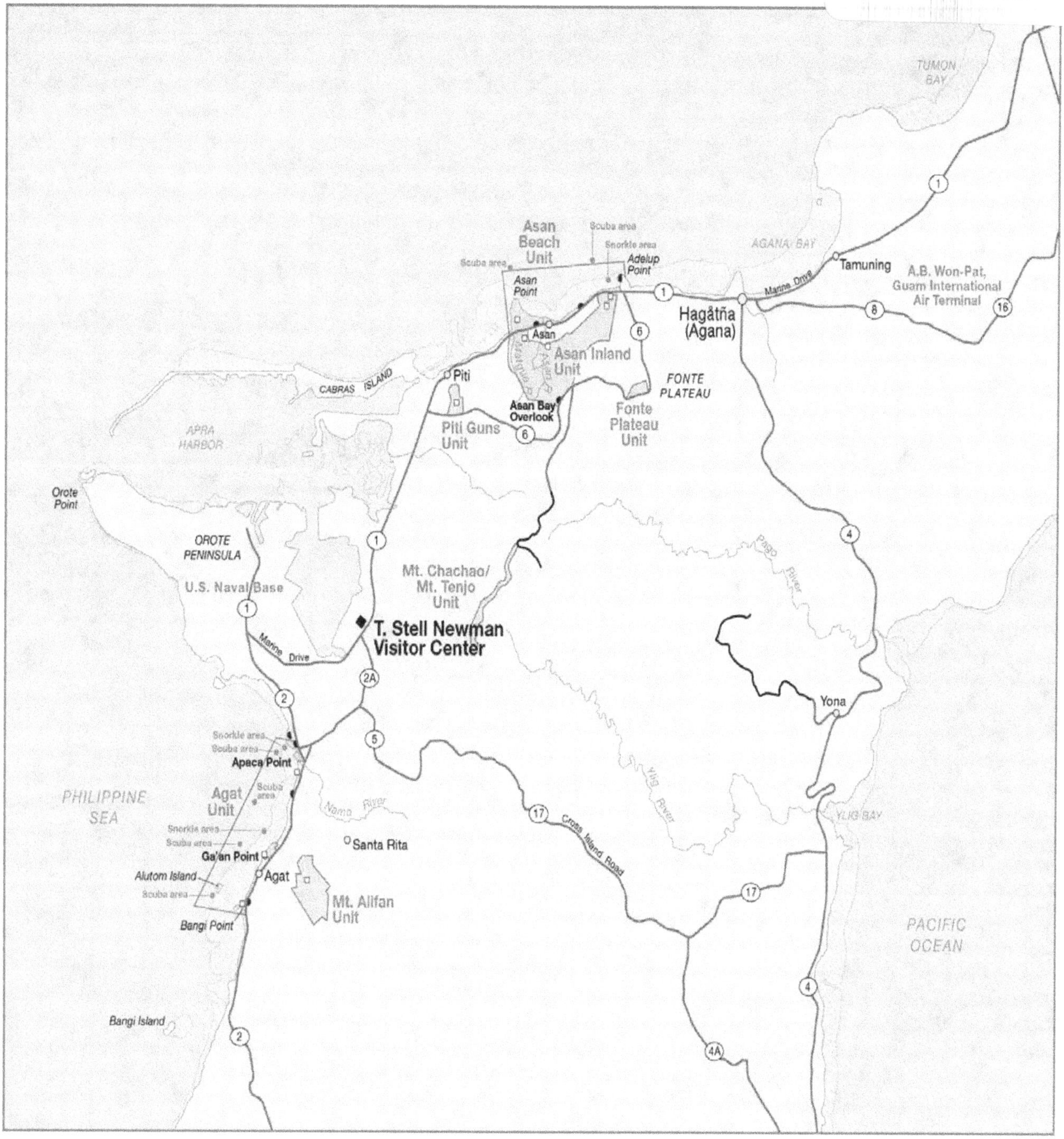

TUMON BAY

AGANA BAY

Asan Beach Unit

Scuba area

Snorkle area

Scuba area

Adelup Point

Asan Point

Tamuning

A.B. Won-Pat, Guam International Air Terminal

Marine Drive

Asan

Hagåtña (Agana)

Asan Inland Unit

FONTE PLATEAU

CABRAS ISLAND

Piti

APRA HARBOR

Asan Bay Overlook

Piti Guns Unit

Fonte Plateau Unit

Orote Point

OROTE PENINSULA

U.S. Naval Base

Mt. Chachao/ Mt. Tenjo Unit

Pago River

Yona

◆ T. Stell Newman Visitor Center

Marine Drive

PHILIPPINE SEA

Snorkle area
Scuba area

Apaca Point

Agat Unit

Scuba area

Nama River

Cross Island Road

Yus River

YLIG BAY

Snorkle area
Scuba area

Ga'an Point

Santa Rita

Alutom Island

Scuba area

Agat

Mt. Alifan Unit

PACIFIC OCEAN

Bangi Point

Bangi Island

War in the Pacific National Historical Park

War in the Pacific National Historical Park
American Memorial Park

Museum Management Planning Team

Kent Bush
Regional Curator, Retired
Pacific West Region
Bellevue, Washington

Tammy Ann Duchesne
Chief, Cultural Resources
War in the Pacific National Historical Park/American Memorial Park
Hagåtña, Guam

Steve Floray
Curator
Pacific West Region
Thousand Oaks, California

Diane Nicholson, Regional Curator
Pacific West Region
Oakland, California
(Team Leader)

Scott Pawlowski
Curator
USS *Arizona* Memorial
Honolulu, Hawai'i

Deb Sheppard
Museum Technician
Hawai'i Volcanoes National Park
Hawai'i Volcanoes, Hawai'i

Brigid Sullivan Lopez
Chief Conservator
Northeast Museum Services
Lowell, Massachusetts

**Department of the Interior
National Park Service
Pacific West Region
2008**

War in the Pacific National Historical Park
American Memorial Park

Museum Management Plan

Recommended by:

Diane L. Nicholson
Regional Curator, Pacific West Region

Jan 5, 2009
Date

Concurred by:

M. Sarah Creachbaum
Superintendent, War in the Pacific National Historical
Park and American Memorial Park

Jan 22, 2009
Date

Approved by:

Jonathan B. Jarvis
Regional Director, Pacific West Region

Feb 3, 2009
Date

Executive Summary

This museum management plan for the museum and archival collections at War in the Pacific National Historical Park (WAPA), located on the island of Guam, and American Memorial Park (AMME), located on the Island of Saipan in the Commonwealth of the Northern Marianas, identifies the key collection management issues facing the parks at this time, and presents a series of recommendations to address those issues. This plan was developed by a team of experienced museum and archival collections management professionals working in cooperation with the parks' management team and staff.

The museum collections at War in the Pacific National Historical Park and American Memorial Park began soon after the parks were authorized and they have grown over the years, especially at WAPA. However, collecting has been somewhat indiscriminate and the current chief of Cultural Resources has been systematically reviewing the collections and deaccessioning those that are inappropriate, out of scope, or no longer have discernable value (i.e., rusted beyond recognition). The objects in the landscape, such as guns and torpedoes, have been accessioned as museum objects instead of being placed as structures on the List of Classified Structures (LCS) or on the Cultural Landscape Inventory as features of the landscape.

The super-typhoon Pongsona (December 2002) destroyed the WAPA visitor center and caused the museum collection to be placed in storage for five years. In 2007, the park moved into a new facility that houses the park visitor center and museum collections management in a renovated former Army Reserve Center. The movement of the collection allowed for the completion of a 100% inventory and the examination of every object. Despite years in a secure building but with inadequate space, the collection is in relatively good condition and a Collection Condition Survey (CCS) is not needed at this time. This new facility contains ample space and allows for the preservation of the collections although some concerns about the building need to be addressed. The AMME Visitor Center is also new and houses exhibits and a theater. The exhibits include a number of museum objects as well as historic objects that were acquired for the exhibit but not accessioned or cataloged into the museum collection. While they are in a less protected environment than the items in the museum collection, they are historic objects and should be accessioned and cataloged into the collection to maintain information on them. The exhibit also needs some upgrading of security, both operational and systems.

The chief of Cultural Resources has been very organized in requesting funding and documenting the parks' needs. The parks' Scope of Collection Statements are in need of revision and refinement but offer some guidance. In the last year, a Museum Preservation Maintenance Plan and a Collections Access Policy were developed. In 2005, a Museum Emergency Operations Plan for AMME was completed in-house but some refinement is needed. In FY 2008, in addition to the Museum Management Plan, Museum Integrated Pest Plans are being completed. In FY 2009, although currently in the program for a CCS, the park will be requesting to change to a Museum Emergency Operations Plan for WAPA as a higher priority, given the possibility of natural disasters (e.g., typhoons, tsunamis, and earthquakes) in this area of the Pacific.

Overall the parks are in relatively good shape due to the energy and organizational abilities of the chief of Cultural Resources. This plan offers guidance in refining the program and makes suggestions to improve the parks' museum programs.

Key Recommendations

These are key program recommendations; more detailed action recommendations follow each issue section of the MMP.

- Improve security and safety of park facilities to ensure continued preservation of the museum collections on display and in storage.

- Develop and institute a park-level policy and plan for the orderly movement of park records into the park archives so that a permanent record of staff management and stewardship of park resources is maintained.

- Establish a preservation maintenance program for the historic weapons, other World War II objects, and monuments throughout the park, including the creation of an exhibit specialist position.

- Continue to develop the museum program, including budgeting and programming documents, to provide an expanded program to preserve, protect, and interpret cultural and natural resources of the parks.

List of Illustrations

List of Tables

Table of Contents

Figure 1 Americans, vehicles, and equipment on beach, WAPA 2579-028

Figure 2 First American flag over Guam, WAPA 2910 (Nat Arch 127-N-63472)

Within the Pacific West Region, the Museum Management Plan (MMP) replaces the Collection Management Plan (CMP) referred to in National Park Service publications such as the Outline for Planning Requirements; *DO#28: Cultural Resource Management*; and the *NPS Museum Handbook*. Whereas the CMP process generally concentrates on the technical aspects of archival and museum operations, the MMP recognizes that specific directions for these technical aspects already exist in the *NPS Museum Handbook* series.

The MMP process therefore does not duplicate that information. Instead it places archival and museum operations in a holistic context within park operations by focusing on how collections may be used by park staff to support specific park goals. This plan recognizes that there are many different ways in which archives, libraries, and museum collections may be organized, linked, and used within individual parks, and as a result provides park-specific advice on how this may be accomplished within this specific unit. Where necessary, material found in the *NPS Museum Handbook* or *Conserve-O-Gram* series will be referenced in the text, and where required, technical recommendations not covered will appear as appendices to this plan.

War in the Pacific National Historical Park (WAPA) was created by 95 Stat. 492 (16 USC 410cc) on August 18, 1978 "In order to commemorate the bravery and sacrifice of those participating in the campaigns of the Pacific theater of World War II and to conserve and interpret outstanding natural, scenic, and historic values and objects on the island of Guam...." Subsequent acts increased the lands administered by the park and authorized the creation of "...a monument which shall commemorate the loyalty of the people of Guam and the heroism of the American forces that liberated Guam." (107 Stat. 2302) This act also requires the preservation and protection of the World War II vintage weapons and fortifications that are within the boundaries of the park. The park has developed a visitor center and museum collections management facility located in a former Army Reserve Center adjacent to U.S. Naval Base Guam. This facility replaces the visitor center that was destroyed by super-typhoon Pongsona in December 2002.

In 1976, Public Law 94-241 (90 STAT. 274) included the authorization of a park on Saipan, and a parcel of land was made available to the Government of the Northern Mariana Islands for the purpose of "...an American memorial park to honor the American and Marianas dead in the World War II Marianas Campaign." This project was to be funded by $2 million received from the Government of the United States for lease of the land and was to be placed in a trust fund to be used for the development and maintenance of the park. American Memorial Park (AMME) was authorized as an affiliated area of the National Park Service under Public Law 95-348 (92 STAT. 492) "...for the primary purpose of honoring the dead in the World War II Mariana Islands campaign." The NPS has developed a memorial and visitor center at Garapan.

War in the Pacific National Historical Park is located on the island of Guam, a territory of the United States. Guam is located 5,800 miles west of the San Francisco Bay Area and 8,300 miles west of Washington, D.C. It is beyond the International Dateline and is thus 15 hours ahead of the Washington office and 18 hours ahead of the Pacific West Regional Office located in Oakland, California. In addition, AMME and WAPA are jointly administered. AMME is located on the island of Saipan about a 50 minute flight away. National Park staff are located on both islands. These logistics make for complications in management of the parks.

With the exception of the objects on display in the AMME Visitor Center, all collections are located in the T. Stell Newman Visitor Center at WAPA. Collections management is located in the renovated building which has new finishes and systems. The collections are stored in a wing of an Army Reserve Center that once included a firing range. There is adequate space for storage and research as well as work space for the park staff. This facility in located in a building under Navy jurisdiction; the lease between the Navy and the NPS is for five years with an option to renew for another five years. This MOU also allows for revocation to the

Navy with 30 days notice. The park is pursuing a 20-year lease but the lease requires the approval and signature of the Secretary of the Navy. This is of particular concern given the buildup expected in the next five years with the movement of 8,000 Marines from Okinawa to Guam. Although WAPA currently enjoys a good relationship with the Navy, and the location of the facility adjacent to the Guam Naval Base could be considered positive for both agencies, the park could possibly be displaced because of changing Admirals at the base.

Park museum staff includes two people: the chief of Cultural Resources (GS-1015-11), who spends about 25% of her time on museum collections, and a .5 FTE GS-025-05 SCEP, who is involved in cataloging, housekeeping, monitoring, and other collections management duties. The latter position is partially funded through projects.

Although this plan covers two parks, War in the Pacific National Historical Park and American Memorial Park, and there are two museum collections, they are both managed by one staff and stored at WAPA. The current collection size as reported in the parks' Collections Management Reports (CMR) for 2007 is about 12,000 items. These figures, however, do not include several historic items purchased for the AMME Visitor Center exhibit or archives that might be discovered after an archives survey of park records. These parks were created to commemorate both the bravery and the sacrifices of those involved in the Pacific war as well as to conserve and interpret outstanding natural and scenic resources. The natural resources collections are expected to increase as research continues.

Park	Archeology	Ethnology	History	Archives	Biology	Total
AMME	41		540			581
WAPA	513	8	5,471	4,483	796	11,271
TOTAL	554	8	6,011	4,483	796	11,852

Table 1 Museum collections as of October 1, 2007, from the 2007 Collections Management Reports

The park is in a good position to continue to maintain the collections. The move into the new facility at the T. Stell Newman Visitor Center has placed the collection in a location that provides preservation and protection of the objects. The staff has established a good track record of using their funding wisely and has completed appropriate documentation for the need for additional base and project funds.

The park staff and the MMP team worked together over the course of the site visit to develop the issue statements contained in this plan. Topics addressed meet the specific needs of War in the Pacific National Historical Park and American Memorial Park as discussed during those meetings, and thus do not necessarily represent a complete range of collections management concerns. Elements of this plan are developmental in nature. The recommendations are intended to guide the park through the process of refining and expanding the existing museum management program that supports all aspects of park operations, while at the same time providing guidelines for the growth and development of the museum management program. This plan is designed to assist the staff in continuing this process for the next five to seven years.

Members of the MMP team were selected for their ability to address specific needs and concerns of the park. Primary information gathering and the initial draft were developed over a two-week period in March 2008.

The team wishes to thank Superintendent Sarah Creachbaum and the staff of War in the Pacific National Historical Park and American Memorial Park for the courtesy, consideration, and cooperation extended during this planning effort. In particular, the team would like to thank James Oelke, WAPA, and Nancy Kelchner and Bryan Piercy, AMME, for their hospitality. Their time, efforts, and involvement greatly facilitated the work, and are very much appreciated. These individuals obviously are dedicated and committed to the preservation of park resources, and it is a pleasure to work with such professionals.

History of
Collection Management

American Memorial Park

American Memorial Park contains 133 acres of land. The park is located on the island of Saipan, which is 110 miles north of Guam, 1,500 miles south of Japan, and 3,340 miles west of Hawaii. American Memorial Park's origin is in Public Law 94-241, dated March 24, 1977, a Covenant to Establish the Commonwealth of the Northern Mariana Islands. This law states:

> "…the United States will make available to the Government of the Northern Marianas Islands 133 acres (54 hectares) at no cost. This property will be set aside for public use as an American memorial park to honor the American and Marianas dead in the World War II Mariana Campaign. The $2 million received from the Government of the United States for the lease of this property will be placed in a trust fund, and used for the development and maintenance of the park in accordance with the Technical Agreement."

On August 18, 1978 (P.L. 95-348), the United States Congress authorized and directed the United States National Park Service (NPS), "to develop, maintain, and administer the existing American Memorial Park…for the primary purpose of honoring the dead in the World War II Mariana Islands Campaign."

The mission of American Memorial Park (AMME) is "to honor the American and Marianas people who died in the World War II Marianas Campaign. As a 'living memorial', the park also creates a venue for community recreational, cultural, and historic activities."

AMME is an affiliated park under the direction of the superintendent on Guam. At the time of the writing of this plan, AMME had only nine accessions. AMME's first artifacts (AMME 1 and AMME 2) were two statues donated by the Bishop Museum in Honolulu in 1990. AMME's third accession was a photo album containing 293 black and white photos donated in 1994. AMME-0004 was AMME's largest and without a doubt the messiest accession.

AMME-0004 has its origins in the Historical Society of American Memorial Park, a non-profit group that existed in Saipan. According to the "History of American Park" article written in the Grand Opening pamphlet for the American Memorial Park Visitor Center, "The old Saipan Museum had closed years before, but out of the 50th Commemoration committees came the Historical Society of the American Memorial Park, which occupied the old Saipan Museum building. This non-profit organization was to last another four years, finally closing the doors of this old museum permanently in 1998."

A General Management Plan (December 1989) also mentions the Saipan Museum. "A 'Saipan Museum' has operated in an existing building within the park from the mid 1980s to 1986. It was run by volunteers and contained interior displays of artifacts, photos, and clippings. Outside of the building, a few Japanese tank hulks and various guns and armament items are exhibited. The museum no longer operates. Lack of funds, termites, and Typhoon Kim did it in."

While the GMP deemed the "Saipan Museum" operated on park land as "done in," a letter from Rex Fullmer, Secretary of the Historical Society of American Memorial Park (dated 12/31/1997) indicated that "all materials and artifacts are given unconditionally and are to be used by the National Park Service as you deem appropriate."

Within the accession files of AMME-0004 are four Deeds of Gift: 1) Materials for inclusion in the Museum Collection, 2) Library Materials Transferred to American Memorial Park, 3) Display and Misc. Materials transferred to American Memorial Park, and 4) a list of office furniture and financial/ administrative records of the HSAMP. Also located within the accession files of AMME-0004 was a copy of a Trip Report and General Recommendations written by Museum Technician Steve Keane to the superintendent. This correspondence details the conditions that existed in the building and the condition of some of the artifacts that were discovered. Keane said of the collection:

Overall, the HSAMP collection, while not spectacular in any sense, would be a worthwhile addition to the rather thin collections of the American Memorial Park. The three-dimensional objects in the collection are not numerous, and would not require a large amount of storage space. Future interpretive exhibits created from park collections would rely heavily on the photographic images and supplementary documentation, while judiciously chosen objects, perhaps supplemented from WAPA's collections, could provide visual punctuation to the displays.

It appears that following the inventory and the signing of the deed of gift, the majority of those objects that were transferred to AMME were then relocated to the curatorial storage facility on Guam.

In 2003, once War in the Pacific NHP had regained some type of normalcy following the super-typhoon, work began in selecting artifacts for the new American Memorial Park Visitor Center and museum. After several years of planning and construction, the museum was opened on Saturday, May 28th, 2005. The exhibits are comprised of a combination of artifacts from the AMME collection, the WAPA collection, and AMME-0009 (a loan of more than two dozen artifacts from the Commonwealth of the Northern Mariana Islands Museum of History and Culture.)

Once the museum was opened during Memorial Day weekend in 2005, Museum Curator Tammy Duchesne finally had the time and budget to search for the several AMME artifacts pertaining to AMME-0004 that could not be located at WAPA. When she located some of the oversized artifacts that were apparently not shipped to WAPA in 1997 or 1998, she also noted that several of the artifacts (mortars, magazine clips, grenades, cartridges, and shells) were in fact live ammunition. Of these live ordinance, all but two cartridges (AMME 68) were uncataloged. Upon discovering the live ammunition, the curator, under instruction of the superintendent, called Emergency Ordinance Disposal. The Saipan police and U.S. Navy Explosive Ordnance Disposal (EOD) personal came to the park and confiscated those items for disposal. They were subsequently deaccessioned.

When Duchesne made contact with a former member of the Historical Society of American Memorial Park in 2008 to learn more about their organization, the member explained to Duchesne that she and many of the members used to hike through the jungle, grasslands, and lands being cleared in search of "surface finds." Essentially, almost all of AMME-0004 consists of objects that were found by treasure hunters. No documentation accompanies any of these objects because they were essentially scavenged. AMME-0004 is AMME's largest accession and one of the few that is not simply photos, clippings, or paintings, so the lack of documentation is regrettable.

AMME-0005 consists of photos donated by a Saipan veteran. AMME-0006 and AMME-0007 were donated by the sons of veterans who served in Saipan during WWII. AMME-0008 consists of paintings depicting WWII action donated by famed WWII (airplane) nose-artist Hal Olsen. AMME- 0009 is an incoming loan of artifacts from the Commonwealth of the Northern Mariana Islands (CNMI) Museum of History and Culture, all of which were on display at the AMME Visitor Center until May 2008 when they were taken off exhibit and returned to the CNMI museum. They will remain with there until the AMME power issues can be resolved.

While many of the objects in the AMME collection are far from noteworthy, in 2007 all the remaining objects in the AMME collection were transported to the curatorial facility in Guam. AMME lacks an appropriate storage facility and with the curator-of -record and the park ranger stationed on Guam, it made sense to consolidate the two parks' collections onto one island.

Considering that the majority of WAPA and AMME collections were in emergency storage from January 2003 until summer 2007, a lot of record reviewing and cataloging is still to be completed. AMME's Scope of Collection Statement is narrower (focusing strictly on the Mariana Islands campaign) than WAPA's (focusing on all the battles in the Pacific Theater), so it is to be expected that the AMME collection would be smaller than the WAPA collection. But every effort should be made to acquire objects that could improve the AMME collection. Finding objects that may have been used before the war in an indigenous home would be especially desirable. Locating handicrafts, basketry, or artwork produced by the indigenous people of the Mariana Islands while they were in the camps following WWII would also be useful. Acquiring such artifacts would allow AMME to return the objects currently on loan to the NPS from the Commonwealth of the Northern Mariana Islands Museum of History and Culture. If the loan were not renewed, NPS would be challenged to find appropriate replacement artifacts for the current exhibits.

AMME and WAPA chief of Cultural Resources and Curator-of-Record Tammy Duchesne are eager to strengthen the current relationship between AMME and the Commonwealth of the Northern Mariana Islands Museum of History and Culture. An effort is under way to convince the CNMI museum to agree to lend NPS ethnographic objects for the upcoming WAPA museum.

War in the Pacific National Historical Park

War in the Pacific National Historical Park was established on August 18th, 1978. It was authorized by Public Law 95- 348, Section 6 to "commemorate the bravery and sacrifice of those participating in the Pacific Theater of World War II and to conserve and interpret the outstanding natural, scenic, and historical values and objects on the island of Guam for the benefit and enjoyment of present and future generations."

The first superintendent, T. Stell Newman (for which the WAPA Visitor Center and curatorial facility is named), arrived on Guam in mid-January 1979. The superintendent was enthusiastic, energetic, and well-liked on the island. According to the WAPA Administrative History, shortly after his arrival, Newman was determined to begin collecting oral histories and searching for artifacts of all kinds that might be donated and used to interpret the War in the Pacific. Throughout the year, he was approached by several individuals wishing to donate a wide assortment of both Japanese and American World War II artifacts. In a December 26, 1979, letter to the chief of military history for the Army in Washington, D.C., Newman asked about the availability of World War II uniforms and the existence of vintage Japanese vehicles that may have been given to the U.S. Army for museum displays (p. 121).

It was Newman's vision that these uniforms be worn while park rangers gave guided tours and lectures. His desire to gather WWII uniforms and artifacts was not fleeting, as it was reported that "Newman's quest for interpretive objects and his tenacity in asking others for them blossomed in 1980. The local news media eagerly continued to support his efforts by routinely printing articles about the latest artifacts discovered in the park or donated to it. Newman's enthusiasm and resourcefulness in locating and acquiring materials for interpretive exhibits were boundless." (p. 122) While he was interested in acquiring all types of artifacts, he was most interested in large military hardware like landing crafts, tanks, artillery pieces, and aircraft. Letters from Newman proved his interest in acquiring a Japanese Zero aircraft and the *Enola Gay*.

Given Newman's interest in the hardware of war, it is not surprising that the first donation was made in late February 1980. WAPA 1 is a1944 Caterpillar Road grader- Model 12 that was donated by Black Construction Company. WAPA's first cataloged artifact was used by Navy Seabees in the Pacific Theater and used later for earth moving activities within the park. Unfortunately, the grader rusted in place and ended up in the dump. The loss of this grader has been a painful lesson for the park: accepting objects means they must be able to care for them.

Newman was also very concerned about presenting an accurate, authentic, and balanced interpretation of the Pacific war: "He was committed to presenting both the Japanese and the American viewpoints on the war. Exhibiting and interpreting Japanese items of military equipment was absolutely essential for presenting a balanced approach to an interpretation of the war in the Pacific." (p.124) He also anticipated and encouraged park visitation by Japanese and even went to Japan to meet with park planners about park development and to seek "advice on the sensitivities of WWII parks for Japanese visitors." (p. 124) He actively asked the Japanese officials he made contact with for any Japanese artifacts and while they were eager to assist, they informed him that there wasn't much left after the war. While he was actively seeking large "hardware" objects as well as Japanese artifacts, he was nonetheless delighted at the acquisition of black and white photos taken by a Marine on Guam.

The arrival of Interpretive Specialist James Miculka in 1980 only accelerated Newman's interest in acquiring artifacts and creating exhibits. By the end of 1980, Miculka attended a curatorial methods training and was therefore the first defacto "museum technician" at WAPA. Miculka was eager to develop an interpretive exhibit. The ability to create exhibits was made possible in 1981 when WAPA moved its administrative office from the Pacific Daily News building to the Haloda Building in Asan. This new location afforded space for interpretive exhibits on the first floor.

The exhibit designing process was aided immensely when in October 1981, Tadao Nakata, a Japanese collector, donated 546 items. This donation (WAPA-0009) is one of WAPA's largest accessions. It finally enabled WAPA to interpret the Japanese perspective that was missing. On July 20, 1982, the efforts of Miculka and Newman were realized with the opening of the visitor center, which would pave the way for WAPA's future exhibits.

On December 27, 1982, Stell Newman met an untimely death when he was killed in a car accident less than one quarter of a mile from the visitor center. While WAPA's first superintendent and museum advocate may have died, WAPA's museum collection would continue to grow even though it might not have always been in the forefront of people's minds during the next decade.

The early years of park development had limited staff and funding. The chief of Interpretation took on many additional duties such as operational needs, managing park resources including the museum collection, and serving as acting superintendent following the unfortunate death of Superintendent T. Stell Newman. For ten years (1980-1990), James Miculka was instrumental in moving the park forward with direct involvement in its development at all levels.

In February 1983, the recently completed Interim Interpretive Plan did list developing a Collection Management Plan as a priority (p.151) but a

Natural and Cultural Resource Management Plan that was written in 1984 (it was expanded from the GMP) failed to list the protection of museum items as being one of its top 16 priorities. (p.138) While the museum collection was not specifically addressed in project statements, the park's archeology sites and structures were addressed in the Natural and Cultural Resources Management Plan.

In 1982, the park's first museum technician, William Summers, was hired. Until the departure of Steve Keane in 1994, the museum technician position was supervised by the chief of Interpretation. In January 1985, Park Ranger Jimmy Garrido, who took on some of the museum duties under the supervision of the chief of Interpretation, developed WAPA's first Scope of Collection Statement. The writing of this document came after a visit from the Western Regional Curator Dave Forgang. Forgang was horrified at the poor environmental conditions that existed and documented the critical need for a secure storage facility. As the Haloda building was undergoing major renovations, it seemed to be an opportune time to make provisions for a curatorial wing within the second floor.

Forgang stated before the renovation that, "dotted throughout the park are many World War II artifacts, all of which are in various states of poor condition; they are literally rusting away." (p.152) The Scope of Collection Statement indicated that the park should acquire museum objects that related to the Pacific Theater during WWII and it set forward procedures for collecting, categorizing, accessioning, and using the collection. The plan also presented a few restrictions pertaining to park collections, one of which was that War in the Pacific NHP "will accept only those items for which it can provide storage, preservation, and protection under conditions that will assure their availability for museum purposes." (p. 152) By the mid-1980s, the museum collection was moved to the second floor, affording it its own space and slightly better conditions. In January 1991, a Scope of Collection Statement for War in the Pacific NHP was completed under Ralph Reyes' tenure.

In September 5-13, 1991, under the leadership of Regional Curator Jonathan Bayless of the Western Regional Office, a team was formed to assist WAPA in the development of its Collection Management Plan.

Members met with park staff and community members during this process. The park was later provided a Trip Report and a draft Collection Management Plan (including a draft for the Conservation of Artifacts located on Guam). However, the plan was never completed nor approved.

On August 28, 1992, Typhoon Omar scoured the island. The typhoon broke three large windows and reportedly flooded the entire administration area. Most of the island, including WAPA, was without power for two months. A generator, purchased after the storm, was shipped from Honolulu. The museum was without climate control while it was waiting for the generator to arrive.

In May, 1993 Sean Cahill accepted the position of museum technician. Cahill had previously worked at Fort Douglas Military Museum in Utah, as a museum technician in the Alaska Regional Office of the NPS, at Grand Canyon, and at Scotty's Castle in Death Valley. He was the first person to arrive at WAPA who had already been trained in museum management methods.

Steve Keane joined the WAPA staff as the park's new museum technician in 1994. He had worked previously at the NPS Western Archeological and Conservation Center (WACC). He left in 2000, and his tenure of 6 years was the longest time someone had spent in the museum technician position. Keane did meticulous work while at WAPA. He was responsible for the organization of the WAPA's first collection storage area, he helped prepare the exhibits at the Haloda building, migrated all the catalog data from hard copies to the first ANCS+ database, kept immaculate records, cataloged the majority of the artifacts for WAPA and AMME, moved almost all the objects from AMME to WAPA, and diligently performed housekeeping tasks. The condition of the artifacts in the WAPA and AMME collection and the quality of the documentation for these items is a testament to the tremendous work done by Keane during his tenure at WAPA. The collection was fortunate to have such a diligent, professional, and conscientious museum technician during much of the 1990s.

After the departure of Steve Keane, Superintendent Karen Gustin and the chief of Interpretation met to discuss the museum technician position and future park needs. They decided that the position should be expanded to take on more cultural resource responsibilities and it would be moved from the Division of Interpretation to the supervision of the superintendent.

On December 16, 1997, Typhoon Paka hit the island and directly impacted WAPA with its loss of electrical power and the consequential threat to artifacts and furnishings. During the storm, "wind tore off a basement door facing the water, which resulted in severe damage to carpets, exhibit cases, and exhibits not only from flooding, but also from actual wave action to which the bottom floor was exposed. The roof of the building was also damaged." (p. 172)

In January 2001, Ana Dittmar arrived at WAPA as the museum curator. She occupied this position for less than two years. In August 2001, Tammy Duchesne began working with the collection as a part time employee for the Arizona Memorial Museum Association (AMMA). Over the months the position would essentially evolve into a museum technician position funded by the cooperating association.

In 2002, two boxes of cataloged archives were returned to WAPA from WAAC. These two boxes contained the cataloged administrative history records for WAPA and AMME, the only cataloged items in the archive discipline for WAPA or AMME. WAPA and AMME need to have surveys completed to uncover which items should be archived.

Eight map cases of large-format archival materials remain uncataloged at WAPA. Apparently no previous museum technician or curator felt comfortable addressing the archive issue. Current staff also lacks training and expertise in archival methods but this will be mitigated this year with the current park ranger/museum technician slated to attend archives training.

In July of 2002, Typhoon Chat'an struck the island of Guam. While most of the island was without power, the visitor center did have access to the generator which enabled the building to remain air conditioned. While the building was air conditioned, the temperature and RH were higher than under normal power circumstances.

Ana Dittmar left WAPA in autumn of 2002. Duchesne who had been working as a museum technician was to be the acting curator until the position was formally filled. Duchesne's part time (24 hours a week) salary was still slated to be funded by AMMA rather than NPS.

Typhoon Chat'an raised havoc in the park, but super-typhoon Pongsona, the most violent and destructive storm in Guam's history, changed WAPA's future. The storm, which was supposed to go north to Saipan, ended up passing directly over the island of Guam. The winds were 165 mph sustained with gusts to 185 mph; the winds and rain battered the island for almost 12 hours. Tornado and lightening activity was also reported. The Haloda building, which had been pounded in the past by scores of typhoons, finally succumbed during super-typhoon Pongsona. The building's electrical panel had been inundated with sea water, which prohibited the staff from running the air conditioner or setting the alarm. Furthermore, engineers suspected that the force of the waves crashing against the load-bearing columns and pillars in the parking lot might have made the building structurally unsound. The immense devastation island-wide and the lack of gasoline on-island because fires raged out of control at the port's fuel tanks forced park staff to stay home for one week under administrative leave. Meanwhile the building was inspected and power lines, thrown cars, jet skis, and other debris were removed from the streets.

When the staff was finally able to return to work and inspect the building, Superintendent Eric Brunnemann informed the staff that they would begin evacuating the Haloda building immediately since it was questionable if the building was structurally sound or if it would ever be fit for occupancy. More than six months would be required to reconfigure the wiring for the building and during the interim, it would be impossible to run a generator. He informed Duchesne, still an AMMA contractor who had been with the park for over a year, that she was responsible for all aspects of the evacuation of the museum artifacts in storage and on exhibit.

During the next two weeks, Duchesne gave direction as she, park staff, emergency hires, and even community service workers worked around the clock to move the collection from the second floor of the Haloda building to emergency and temporary storage at Sirena Plaza, the US Attorney's building in Hagåtña. Shrink wrap and other archival supplies were flown in from Harper's Ferry and the collection was moved in the park's caravan, the park's Ford Explorer, and personal vehicles. The collection, cabinets, and shelving were moved into two small, carpeted rooms and the collection remained there from January 2003 until June 2007. These two small rooms also contained all the artifacts, cabinetry, shelving, and all the books and magazines from the WAPA library. During this time, the majority of the collection was inaccessible. The crowded conditions made monitoring, inventories, and cataloging virtually impossible for over four years.

Shortly after the collection had been successfully moved without using outside labor or vehicles, Brunnemann offered Duchesne a SCEP position with the park while she completed her degree. In May 2004 when Duchesne completed her thesis and graduated with her MA in Micronesian Studies, she was converted to a GS-05 Museum Curator. She later went on to complete the Certificate Program in Museum Studies from the George Washington University.

Unfortunately, the situation at WAPA following the typhoon, as well as other management priorities at the park, resulted in the museum curator not being involved in the early development of AMME's exhibit planning and design. When freed from other management priorities, Museum Curator Tammy Duchesne later joined the team.

In 2004, the Inventory and Monitoring program came to WAPA to collect samples of the plants that exist in the park. This effort resulted in the collection of over 700 plant specimens. These specimens formed the beginning of the WAPA herbarium, and along with a few coral specimens and two stuffed turtles comprise the natural history collection. With an ecologist on staff since 2000, the natural history portion of the museum collection will possibly grow.

In June 2007, thanks to MCPPP funds, the collection was moved from emergency storage to its current location with the help of two curators from the Pacific West Region, Duchesne, and James Oelke, a WAPA SCEP park ranger with museum responsibilities. The collection now resides in the T. Stell Newman Visitor Center in Sumay. The collection storage space contains no windows and can only be accessed from the curatorial office. To enter the storage area, a code must be entered. A building-wide alarm system is also in place and typhoon shutters are also present on all windows and doors. This new building affords the collection adequate protection from theft and environmental disasters.

WAPA's collection has not had an easy life. It was without a Scope of Collection Statement for the first six years and did not have a person with museum training on staff until 1993, fifteen years after the park was established. In addition to lacking direction and qualified trained staff, the collection was also housed in inadequate facilities which resulted in a few moves and several instances of its being without climate control following natural disasters. Clearly, in Guam's salt air and tropical climate, any collection is in jeopardy if there is no power, HVAC system, or generator in place. The collection was also forced into "dead storage" for several years while WAPA staff tried to locate suitable spaces for offices, a visitor center, and a collection storage facility. WAPA's museum program has been plagued by under-trained staff, poor facilities unsuited for the multitude of natural disasters that can occur, a high turnover of staff (often with large lapses between positions), a shortage of funding during the parks first 25 years, and a general lack of continuity in location, staff, or direction.

While WAPA's collection has endured many challenges, its future seems bright. The collection is now housed in an adequate building, and for the first time more than one person is dedicated to the Cultural Resources Division. Duchesne is the permanent chief of Cultural Resources and the curator-of-record for both WAPA and AMME while Oelke is a part time SCEP ranger with curatorial duties. Staffing also seems stable with Oelke still having two years left in his BA and Duchesne content in her position at the park.

The WAPA museum program is further strengthened by Superintendent Sarah Creachbaum and the regional curators, all of whom are very supportive and aware of WAPA's efforts amid the day to day challenges of being located on a small, remote island on the other side of the International Dateline in the western Pacific. The new, strongly-built and adequately-protected T. Stell Newman Visitor Center, the curatorial facility, and the museum management plan that follows will help WAPA improve upon its current museum management program.

Figure 3 T. Stell Newman Visitor Center, WAPA

Museum
Management Philosophy

The basic principles for managing museum collections in national parks are not always well understood. Park managers, resource managers, and interpreters are often too busy with their specialties and daily work to fully consider the concepts and logistics governing collections management. It is easy for parks to fall short of developing a sound museum management program and, as a result, not realize the full benefit and value possible from their collections.

This section provides the following background information about museum collections:

- The purpose of museum collections

- How museum collections represent park resources

- Determining where to locate museum collections

- Establishing access, use, and management policies for collections

- Professionalism in collections management

- Determining the content of museum collections

Purpose of Museum Collections within National Parks

Museum collections always contain objects and specimens, and most parks administer their own archives and operate their own libraries. These functions are necessary to support the work of the organization as a whole. These resources—archives, collections, and libraries—often are accessible to the staff, researchers, and public, but on a controlled basis.

Within national parks, museum collections (including archives) serve four basic functions:

- **Documentation of resources** – Park collections should serve as documentation of the physical resources of the park as well as the history of park efforts to preserve and protect those resources.

- **Physical preservation and protection of resources** – Park collections should help preserve and protect park resources, not only by keeping the specimens and collections documenting the resources, but also by preserving the information about the individual items and the resource as a whole. This is central to the management of both natural and cultural material.

- **Research** – During documentation of collections, a park performs research to provide the background information used in cataloging. The park is also responsible for making this information available to legitimate research, which can itself lead to new discoveries about an individual item, or the park as a whole.

- **Public programs** – The park is responsible for using its collections to provide information to the public. Exhibits, publications, and interpretive programs are traditional means of supplying public information, but new technology has led to other communication methods, including electronic access through web sites and online databases.

How Collections Represent Park Resources

A park's museum, library, and archival collections provide different perspectives on its resources.

- Museum collections, which contain three-dimensional objects and specimens, should represent the resources within the park boundaries. Examples of museum collections include: artifacts from archaeological activities; specimens, objects, and documentation resulting from cultural and natural resource management projects; paint samples and building fragments from restoration of historic structures.

- The park museum archives should contain files, manuscripts, maps, building plans, and photos that document the history of the area and park development, and the management of park resources. Individual collections within the archives should serve to further document the activities that created portions of the museum collections. Examples of park archives include: copies of field journals and maps created while collecting botanical specimens; photographs taken during historic structure work; maps and as-built drawings made during utility installation; and property, land, and water use agreements that document past acquisition and use of park lands.

- The park library should contain both published literature and less formal reports and documents relating to park resources and their management. Examples might include: general literature concerning local history, flora, and fauna; specialized scientific studies relative to biota and historical and archaeological resources found in the park; circulating copies of all park specific planning documents; and trade, craft, and professional journals, reflecting the need for park staff to remain current in their field.

Determining where to Locate Park Collections

The *NPS Museum Handbook* should be used as a guideline for identifying locations of branch or satellite park collections, and establishing methodologies for their documentation, organization, storage, and use.

Centrally located collections are often the most effective since this promotes efficient use of space (particularly in terms of combining preparation and work areas). However, it may also be efficient operationally to split the collections among potential users (for example, the herbarium and insect collection going to separate branches for storage and use).

Branch or satellite collections are possible as long as proper preservation and security conditions are met, and the requisite work areas necessary for management and use are provided. Overall responsibility for documentation, preservation, and reporting should, however, remain vested in one curatorial lead position, no matter where branch collections are located.

Establishing Access, Use and Management Policies

Access, use, and management policies define who can access the collections (both staff and public), what types of use are possible and under what conditions, and how the collections should be managed.

Desired outcomes or products should be identified as well, for example, the types of services that are desired by staff from the collections manager. Some examples might include production of over-lays for buried utilities; production of CDs containing research done at the park; liberal access to botanical specimens for comparative studies; and inter-library loan services. Samples of access, use, and management policies may be obtained from the lead curator.

The park may wish to consider the use of focus group or set up a museum program advisory group to develop a number of park-specific documents, including a Role and Function Statement, for the combined collections. These would clearly state who is responsible for the development of a joint resource and how it will function to serve park-wide goals. Access and use policies should be defined and implemented. Responsibilities for development, documentation, and management of the resources should be defined in a formal Position Description and associated performance standards. These objectives must be fully defined in writing if they are to be accomplished in fact.

Professionalism

The management of archival, museum, and library collections requires the application of three different management philosophies and technological approaches. These disciplines each have two components: technical and professional. It is possible to be proficient in either one of these components without being fully functional in the other.

The primary difference between the technical and philosophical lies not only in understanding how to apply the technology, but in being able to determine when, why, and which technologies need to be applied in any given situation. This distinction and ability can be called "professionalism," and, like connoisseurship, it can be an elusive, difficult thing to define— probably because most practitioners of the curatorial craft possess varying degrees of facility with both the technological and philosophical aspects of the work.

Professionalism does need to be practiced and exercised to develop properly. It is better fostered by mentoring, particularly in the early stages, for professionalism is difficult to develop in isolation— it takes fairly intimate association with a range of others of the craft, so that the developing professional personality has a healthy range of philosophy, opinion, and action to model. Professionalism needs to be maintained in much the same manner.

The management of park archives was added to the park curator's portfolio in the mid-1980s. Increasingly, park curators also manage the individual park's library program and, in some cases, records management program. However, the NPS also has archivist positions, a related but specialized profession that provides more guidance and management of park museum archives either at their home parks or through agreement with other parks with such a need. This accretion of complex duties has to some extent resulted from the overall loss of permanent positions within the Service, and particularly within the parks. These factors are not likely to improve in the foreseeable future, so park management must ensure that each position is filled with the best-qualified candidate available.

The professional series and journeyman level for the position of park curator is GS-1015-11 and for the archivist is GS-1420-11. The GS-1016 (museum) or GS-1421 (archives) series is the technician or specialist series, which is not expected to operate independently from professional oversight. A GS-1015-11 or GS-1420-11 is required by qualification standards, service, and regional policy to independently manage a museum program, and administer museum program funds. Parks that do not have this position on staff need to provide this level of oversight through the use of a curator-of-record agreement.

Prospective candidates for professional positions should be selected for a combination of factors including academic study, work experience and subsequent training, membership and activity in professional associations, and remaining current with the professional body of literature. Selection would best be done by a review committee of established professional NPS curators.

The following recommendations should be considered for developing and formalizing the park's management philosophy concerning the management for archives, libraries, and museum collections:

- Create a focus group of senior staff representing all park administrative units to define what the collections should contain, how they should be managed and accessed most efficiently, and what products should be available upon request.

- Define the role and function of the combined collections by formal statement, formal access policies, and formal methodologies for depositing collections material, archival information, and required literature into the collections.

- Identify possible cooperative partnerships within the park network, the professional community, and groups and individuals that hold common interests regarding the preservation and management of park resources.

Figure 4 Museum storage cabinets

Issue Statement

**Appropriate and sustainable maintenance programs are essential for
long-term preservation of museum collections and related cultural
material.**

Background

The equatorial marine environment of Guam presents a formidable
challenge to preservation of all manufactured materials, and particularly,
to objects made of metal. The immutable law of entropy demands that all
material and forms of energy revert to the stable basic compounds from
which they were made, i.e., from metal to stable ore, and this reversion is
assisted by natural forces in the environment: water in the liquid and vapor
state; water and air-borne electrolytic corrosive salts; rampant and
decaying vegetation influencing pH soil conditions; and light and heat
promoting photochemical deterioration of organic-based materials such as
paints and other coatings. Material destruction is also assisted by
biological agents ranging from algae to humans. Preservation of cultural
material is a daunting task on Guam where these natural forces are in
over-drive.

The park understands these challenges and has made considerable
progress toward preservation of the historically significant material both in
the museum collections as well as military equipment left in-situ within
the cultural landscape surrounding events of the Liberation of Guam on
July 21, 1944.

As requested by the park, the first Collection Management Plan in 1991
(unfinished) included a section by Metals Conservator Herbert Bump, a
specialist in conservation of coastal archeological metal, to develop a
Conservation Plan for the severely corroded military artifacts exhibited

outdoors. This was the first assessment of the treatment needs of the remaining coastal defense guns at Ga'an Point and the Japanese guns at the Piti unit. Bump also examined metal objects in the museum collection and recommended treatment procedures of surface cleaning by grit-blasting and electrolytic reduction and by applied protective and coatings. The treatment plan was not enacted because of logistical and funding problems.

By the late 1980s and early 1990s, it was clear that developing on-site expertise in preservation of the outdoor military collection was the most effective way to provide critical maintenance necessary for long-term preservation. In June 1994, in celebration of the fiftieth anniversary of the Liberation, an ambitious 5-day workshop, Conservation Management of Historic Metals in Tropical Environments and sponsored by the National Park Service Cultural Resources Training Initiative and the War in the Pacific NHP, was offered in Guam. The target audience was historic preservation officers from islands in Micronesia including Chuuk, Yap, Palau, Kosrae, Saipan, and Pohnpei. The aim was to educate management and support staff toward intelligent contracting for repair/rehab and conservation projects, but the real need was to educate and train the front-line maintenance staff who bear the responsibility of maintenance of these resources. Instead, the 5-day course included highly technical discussions of corrosion chemistry and treatment selection more appropriate to an audience of trained conservators. As a course practicum, two anti-aircraft guns at Ga'an Point were sandblasted, stabilized, and painted.

Park staff repainted the guns in 1998 and again in 2001, and the Ga'an guns were completely rehabbed by local WWII metals preservation expert John Gerber in 2004. At the time of the MMP site visit, three technical proposals for retreatment of the guns were being evaluated for the preservation contract award in FY 08. Deterioration of the third Piti gun located in an earth revetment is advanced to the point that rehabbing is impractical.

In April 2008, the Navy transferred a rare two-man Japanese midget submarine to the park. The sub was placed on display in front of the visitor center in April 2008 and refurbished in June 2008. The Navy refurbished the 80-foot submarine by contract to Pacific Foundation in 2001. Once installed, John Gerber volunteered his expertise and labor to refurbish the sub in June 2008. Transfer of this complex object increases the preservation maintenance burden of the park.

Three additional guns and eight mines now located in the park maintenance yard need attention as well. Only one gun in this collection has the structural integrity to be useful as a cultural document, but will still require sandblasting and repainting for exhibit and wayside interpretation.

In all of the past and planned treatments, paint color selection remains an important issue for visual authenticity. Honolulu-based Paintings Conservator Laurence Pace was contracted to provide a paint analysis of the Piti Guns and Ga'an guns, but unfortunately, previous sand-blasting left little chance of routine sampling, although in some cases, cross-section analysis remained possible to detect traces of historic paint.

All elements of the bronze Asan Bay Overlook Memorial installed in 1995 are in extremely poor condition due to initial foundry patina issues, lack of maintenance instructions, past inappropriate treatments, the ravages of Pongsona and other typhoons, and by simple neglect.

In anticipation of President Clinton's visit in 1998, abrasive methods including polishing with electric rotary wire wheels were used to "brighten up" the surface of the Memorial's sculptural panels which had become disfigured by corrosion since installation because of the lack of a protective coating on the bronze. With more unprotected metal exposed to the corrosive sea-air, deterioration accelerated, making the artistic narrative of the panels nearly impossible to read. NPS Conservator Brigid Sullivan visited the site in 2001 and stated that the damage was so severe that the sculptural panels would have to be abraded to clean metal with walnut shell grit (not sand), the panels completely re-patinated using lighter-toned patination chemicals, and the surface coated with protective lacquer and waxed to isolate it from corrosive elements.

The name plaques fabricated and installed in 1996 by the Pietro Mussi Foundry on the mainland have also deteriorated substantially since treatment by Sullivan and park maintenance in 2001. Unfortunately, the low-cost copper alloy, milled Muntz metal, selected by Mussi was a poor choice for the exposed Overlook Memorial. Normally, this metal is used in interior applications such as signs in hotels and banks, and cannot be considered suitable for memorials in the full face of weather. During the 2001 site-visit, the panels were disfigured by lifted and opaque polyurethane protective coating and by blackened areas of corrosion where the coating failed. Cleaning and coating techniques were demonstrated to and practiced by park maintenance staff in a 2-day site visit, and the park staff completed the treatment of the remaining panels.

Five years after Pongsona destroyed the previous visitor center, the new T. Stell Newman Visitor Center opened in 2007 at the former Army Reserve Center, located just outside the gates of the U.S. Naval Base. The new facility is an enormous improvement over the former Haloda Building and provides a large (approximately 1,600 sq.ft.) dedicated climate-controlled storage room with adjacent curatorial workroom in the renovated rifle range area. The park has finalized a five-year lease with an option to renew for another five years. The need for a longer-term lease is needed particularly in light of the anticipated increase in development on Guam to begin in 2009. The park and the region will continue to work toward a long-term lease agreement.

Aldrich Pears designed the exhibits at the AMME Visitor Center in Saipan, which was completed in May 2005. The exhibits rely more on super-graphics than museum collection items in interpreting wartime events. Cataloged objects used in the exhibits are enclosed in museum cases with few exceptions. In addition, original World War II items were acquired and placed on sand-like platforms to simulate an active amphibious military landing. These materials should probably be cataloged. New exhibits for the WAPA visitor center are currently being designed by Daniel Quan Design and care should be taken to ensure that the design includes appropriate levels of preservation for the museum collection objects which will be on display.

Discussion

Memorial Weapons

Preservation treatment and subsequent preventive maintenance of guns at Ga'an Point and Piti are highly specialized and few people or companies have professional qualifications and expertise to undertake conservation of these complex objects. Lacking staff expertise, the park must contract for preservation.

Accessing appropriate professional contractors has been quite difficult in the islands, especially in an administrative environment that discourages sole-source contracting —usually the most direct way to ensure professional qualifications and continuity of treatment providers. For example, local WWII metals expert John Gerber has a long demonstrable record of successful treatment of large military equipment on Guam and other military sites, but has no inclination for cumbersome government contracts which are necessary above the allowance of $3,000. However, because the need for preservation treatment and maintenance is cyclical in nature, the park could explore alternatives such as creating an IDIQ to a qualified provider for a five-to seven-year period of scheduled treatment, thereby making tedious contracts unnecessary for each individual treatment campaign.

Ideally, the park should work toward establishing a base-funded position for preservation and treatment oversight of all memorials within the park. This position should logically be in the GS-1010-9/11 Exhibit Specialist series which requires professional preservation training and experience for inclusion. Alternatively, a four-year renewable term position (also exhibit specialist) could be developed and largely, if not entirely, supported by Cultural Cyclic Maintenance funding. The Final Report, WAPA and AMME Organization and Review Operations, does not include any positions in Cultural Resources besides the current museum curator; this position would, however, provide for direct preservation and protection of park resources.

Both the exhibit specialist and the chief of Maintenance should receive updated FMSS training to key into CCM funding cycles and track and schedule cyclical treatments. Documentation of all treatments to memorials is essential for the preservation record, and the best place for this documentation is in the List of Classified Structures data base.

Asan Bay Overlook Memorial Sculptures and Name Plaques

Directly after the 2001 site visit, Brigid Sullivan discussed the Memorial's conservation and shared photographs of the bronze memorial panels with Sculptor Robert Shure of Skylight Studios and the Paul King Foundry in the Boston area, both of whom have worked well in the past with the NPS on similar projects. Treatment options and strategies were discussed from each point of view. Fortuitously, at that time, the Paul King Foundry had a studio in Japan as well as New England, and was (and may still be) able to undertake the on-site stripping, patination, and protective coating; they provided a cost estimate which was relayed to the Seattle office and the new WAPA park superintendent. No action was taken, and with the catastrophic typhoon a few years later, park and regional priorities shifted away from repair of the Asan Memorial.

The park is now in the planning phase for replacement of the name plaques because they were stolen. The park currently has no law enforcement program and memorials throughout the parks are routinely vandalized.

The spatial configuration of Asan Bay Overlook Memorial Sculpture will increase substantially when the Muntz metal plaques are changed out for granite because the stone cannot be incised with the fairly small laser-cut font (about 18-point); it requires a font size of 30 point or more for inscription. In addition, the park has received a list from Congresswoman Bordallo's office containing over 2,000 names that will need to be included. It is recommended that the park work closely with the memorial designers to ensure that no editorial or material errors are made in redesigning the name plaque enclosure.

T. Stell Newman Visitor Center

The park's permanent exhibits are in the planning stage and are scheduled for installation in 2010. At the time of the MMP site visit, only one museum case contained museum objects, none of which were particularly climate or light sensitive. However, the park curator must be closely involved in the final selection of exhibit objects and carefully review how they will be mounted and the type and intensity of the exhibit light levels to circumvent installation mistakes that may promote deterioration of light-sensitive organic material.

The HVAC system serving the visitor center is not ideal for providing museum standards for preservation of museum collections. Monitoring data in the storage room indicate that the system has no reheat capability to stabilize relative humidity, and is programmed to respond to temperature only. The huge deadband zone of RH% fluctuations in comparison to cycling temperatures clearly indicate that there is no air-reheat system to constantly modulate air temperature so that the AC does not cycle completely off when the temperature setting is achieved. This is also an indication of an over-sized unit.

The distractingly loud noise and forced air from the overhead ducts may indicate installation issues as well as the over-sized tonnage causing operation at full force to satisfy thermostat requirements. Fortunately, the collections of WAPA are fairly sturdy vernacular objects that have a wide range of tolerance to fluctuating conditions of temperature and relative humidity, but nonetheless, data logger charts show frequent excursions into RH levels at and above the mold threshold of 70% RH. Mold spores are ubiquitous in tropical climates, and if once hydrated, mold conidiae can fruit out even as low as 50% RH.

WAPA Collections Storage

The museum storage room and curatorial workroom are very well-organized and kept scrupulously clean, but the space is compromised by construction flaws, most notably by the blistered milled sheet flooring indicating possible trapped moisture between the milled linoleum-like floor covering and the cement floor. The previous flooring had been mechanically removed and disposed of as hazardous waste because of asbestos content, and the concrete base thoroughly cleaned before installation of the new floor. Lifted blistered areas in applied sheet coverings generally indicate moisture pockets in the floor ground. Ideally, stable sub-flooring should have been installed to avoid problems of blistering which can become a safety hazard for tripping. Safety and hazard mitigation funding sources may be available to cover the cost. New flooring should definitely be placed over sub-flooring.

The storage room is over 1,600 sq. ft. and more than large enough to accommodate the present collection plus growth. The park will soon receive a moderately-sized collection of military uniforms and paraphernalia (seven large textile boxes) from the Navy. Although the storage area has plenty of space for expansion, the existing cabinetry is not adequate to store all collections to a high museum standard. Mismatched, old (i.e lift-front Lane cabinets) and damaged cabinets should be replaced with standard matched cabinets with functional gaskets and well-engineered drawers and doors.

During the site visit, contents of several double-wide drawers exceeded the weight strength of the drawers themselves, and drawers housing military uniforms and other textiles were often over-packed. These would benefit from decompression and additional internal padding to avoid creasing through gravity weight of multiple fabric layers. The recent Museum Preservation Maintenance Plan (2008) outlines present conditions and provides a list of existing cabinetry in the storage area which will be useful in planning for storage cabinetry upgrades. Moreover, removal of the cabinetry for installation of new flooring for hazard mitigation presents an ideal time to rethink cabinetry needs and placement of collections in locations appropriate to weight, use, fragility and material and the need for expansion in specific material categories.

American Memorial Park, Saipan

Exhibits in the visitor center include paper-based, metal, plastic, wood, and textile-based objects. However, all paper objects, the most climate-sensitive material, are facsimile reproductions. The exhibits are lit with

PAR MR-16 track lights, but because the highly light-sensitive paper-based materials are facsimile reproductions, light levels are not a significant preservation issue. General light levels are low in the exhibit areas. Light monitoring data has been gathered in lumen measurements which refer to lumen output of UV light rather than the more useful measurement of visible light (lux or foot candles). The park has an Elsec 764 light meter, and the curator should record visible light in foot candle or lux measurements to determine if light levels on specific objects fall within or exceed museum standards for various materials. Based on impressions during the MMP site visit to Saipan, the light levels are probably within or not far in excess of the range of acceptability per object material type, but the curator should verify the levels with the Elsec Monitor and make adjustments to track lighting as necessary and possible.

Exhibited objects appeared to be in good condition with the exception of a razor (AMME 42) and a pistol in the Japanese artifacts case which showed active light rusting. These objects were treated and stabilized on-site by the chief of Cultural Resources under direction of the MMP conservator.

The D-Day Saipan exhibits include mock-ups of material left on sand dunes after landing. Some of these objects are historic items and should be placed on a list of accountable property.

Environmental conditions as monitored by the HOBO Onset Datalogger appear to be consistent with preservation standards for museum collections.

Museum project planning

The park has submitted a PMIS project for Collection Condition Surveys for both WAPA and AMME (PMIS 140805). At this point, these surveys are not necessary, and remedial and preventive guidance can be provided in related documents and forms of correspondence.

In PMIS project 122558A &B "Develop Conservation Plan and Maintenance Plan for Management of the War in the Pacific Various Memorials," Component A requests funding of $12,660 for the site visit, and $10,000 for development of the conservation plan. With the anticipated need for scientific testing, Component A should be rounded out to $15,000. This PMIS project is well-conceived and timely and should rank high in park and regional reviews.

Recommendations

- Revisit the parks' organization review document regarding preservation and protection of park resources.

- Develop a GS 9/11 Exhibit Specialist position to organize and oversee memorial preservation at WAPA. Seek OFS increase base funding, or 4-year renewable-term appointment supported by CCM funds.

- Submit a PMIS project for cyclical maintenance of WAPA memorials, including multiples of up to 10 years to keep funding in place.

- Use FMSS to manage cyclic funding and treatment schedules for memorials.

- Use the LCS database to record physical treatment to on-site memorials.

- Pursue ways to access professional conservation services through IDIQ contracts to local experienced treatment providers.

- Ensure that the curator is involved in all exhibits planning involving selection of museum objects and installation issues such as light levels and mounting.

- Plan to proceed with conservation treatment of the damaged Asan Bay Overlook memorial sculptural relief panels.

- Submit a PMIS project to replace unstable flooring in the storage room with Cyclic Maintenance funding.

- Submit a PMIS project to upgrade museum storage cabinets and decompress textile storage with Cultural Cyclic or MCPP funds.

Issue B —
Information Management

Issue Statement

**Identifying, arranging, and processing archival materials that
document park resources and management activities will strengthen
research, promote public dialog, and support park operations.**

Background

WAPA and AMME have an excellent opportunity to design and
implement sound records and archival management strategy. Typhoon
Pongsona in 2002 damaged an undetermined quantity of WAPA's records
which were subsequently disposed of because of mold. Since no
systematic survey of the destroyed records is known, this presumably
included many resource management records of interest to the museum
archives. In the early years of park development (ca. 1983-1988), copies
of all outgoing correspondence were sent to the Pacific Island Director.
Records that may be of importance to park history, development, and/or
preservation efforts may be within that office.

The museum archives has a limited number of archival resources currently
in its collection. It has great potential for growth over the next 4-10 years
as veterans and those with first-hand accounts of WWII die and the
currently held resource management records are added to the museum
archival collection. WAPA currently enjoys the situation of having few
records to manage, but with ample potential for growth in areas key to
achieving its mission. In particular, museum archives should play a part in
future natural and cultural resource management, maintenance, and
administrative decisions and projects. AMME's resource management
records appear more extensive and in better shape because the site has not
suffered through a super typhoon. Both parks have need for a records
management program that will ensure the preservation and protection of
these important resources while taking into account the small size of the

staffs. The remote nature of Guam and Saipan presents numerous challenges to the park curator and other park staff in the areas of procurement, training, natural disasters, and access to peers. This section contains observations and advice to implement solid knowledge management practices that play a roll increasing work productivity, consistency, and proficiency. Information or knowledge management can be viewed as a comprehensive approach to achieving NPS objectives by making use of information. It involves design, review, and implementation of both social and technological processes to improve the application of knowledge in the collective interest of stakeholders.

The park has seen significant levels of continuous employee turnover. The superintendent, chief of Natural Resources, chief of Cultural Resources, chief of Maintenance and two term interpreters are all relatively new to their positions. The park has a number of unfilled, but anticipated, positions. A number of interviewees mentioned the need for advice on managing information resources like digital files, email, and desk files.

Currently, there is no consistent approach to retaining records or preserving electronic images. Some staff uses the central files, others do not. The IT system is not comprehensive enough to back up all electronic files. Email is not being managed as records. Training and situational awareness helps ensure staff makes the best of available resources found in the park. It also develops a consistent manageable approach to records and archival management that maximizes benefits of maintaining records in the first instance.

There is little doubt natural disasters have a significant impact on Guam. During El Niño years, three to five typhoons per year are anticipated. Earthquakes are felt regularly on the island. Tsunamis are a real threat to the low lying visitor centers on Guam and Saipan. In short, any collection located at either park is at risk for flooding, mold, and physical damage. Some amount of risk management is needed to ensure critical archival resources can survive a civil emergency. Risk management is simpler to accomplish with orderly, well-maintained records and archives.

So that most employees understand their responsibilities in park-wide information management, the park must survey and arrange its existing resources to reflect organization history and future needs. The curator has no experience or training in archives, and therefore a professional with in-depth knowledge of theory and practice can maximize the park's efforts, particularly when paired with knowledgeable on-site staff. An outside specialist is also most likely to have the skill sets needed to work across organizational divisions.

A comprehensive approach will be needed to reach the goals in this MMP's recommendations for information resources that are comprehensive in scope, adequately protected for the long term, and easily accessible by stakeholders.

Discussion

Park archives (also referred to as museum archives in this document) serves as a repository for historic records created outside of the park which relate to the park's purpose or its resources, and for park-created records pertaining to the history of park resource management.

A records survey is a systematic effort to locate and identify all the records held in a park unit. Surveys help gain control of existing records and bring them into a managed environment. It can be used to collect information for records inventories, and it can also inform the development or implementation of a retention schedule, filing scheme, and, most importantly, professional recommendations for arrangement.

AMME and WAPA have records and museum archives in storage areas, closets, desks, offices, and other areas throughout the park. AMME has approximately 60 linear feet of records located in the visitor center and administrative offices. Additionally, there are three five-drawer map cases containing both drawings and specifications.

WAPA records are less centralized and mainly consist of division and desk files cared for primarily by division chiefs. Further, there is a significant large format collection consisting of six five-drawer map cases and approximately 30 boxes for rolled storage. Additional rolled maps are in the meeting room closet space. An unknown number of digital photographs and CAD drawings exist with each division chief and on the main server. The WAPA museum archives includes approximately 3600 images, digital files used to create the park's web page, and an initial archival collection consisting of WAPA administrative files described by a WACC archivist. As this is not a survey, further investigations will lead to additional archival resources.

WAPA and AMME-created resource management records are in central files, division files, and desk files but should be considered part of the museum archives collection and brought together into one manageable location. This will require a park-wide survey and arrangement recommendations. Additionally, those resource management records that are inactive should be moved to the museum archives. Historic records exist in a limited amount in the museum collection.

Resource management records typically found in central and desk files include research project reports, associated records such as field notes, and administrative, planning, interpretation, maintenance and history of cultural and natural resources documents. This might include records of land acquisition, planning and development, changing information on park resources, and materials that reflect conditions, use, or modifications of park resources. Official NPS file codes "D," "H," "L," "N," and "Y" contain records of permanent value to park resources.

WAPA and AMME are in slightly different circumstances because of site histories and former management of these records. WAPA had some of their resource management files destroyed by typhoon-caused water damage. AMME's resource management records appear more extensive and in better shape because of the site staff's efforts to keep records dry and use effective records management strategies.

How Records Management Fits Into Museum Archives

Not all records found at AMME and WAPA constitute resource management records. Official records make up the predominant bulk of all records found at both locations. Prior to retiring official records to the

Federal Records Center (FRC – NARA), resource management records will have to be separated and added to the museum collection. Those not retained by the museum will be managed under *NPS-19* by the park's records manager.

The park needs to determine an institutional wide strategy for handling park central files because central files of significant importance need to be managed for the long term and will eventually come under the museum curator.

WAPA's Natural Resource division will be working with the Pacific Islands I&M Network to develop specific protocols for monitoring unit plants and animals. These are anticipated to be tailored to park circumstances. Documenting agency decisions, such as I&M research design, is fundamental to park museum archives. These resource management decisions have long term implications for park resource monitoring. Such decisions also have significant impacts on the validity of research design. An inability to review research design degrades confidence in all research tied to project decisions.

Establishing Archives

If potential archival material is site-related and relevant to the park's Scope of Collection Statement (SOCS), it should be appraised for inclusion in the archives. Archival appraisal involves determining a collection's administrative, artifactual, associational, evidential, informational, and monetary value to the park. This is an argument justified by the SOCS and supported by the material being appraised.

See the *NPS Museum Handbook*, Part II, Appendix D, "Museum Archival and Manuscript Collections" for more information. Guidelines for locating, processing, describing, and providing access to archival collections are presented here and in *Conserve O Grams* 19/15 and 19/16.

Collection Level Arrangement

Archival collections are to be properly described as part of the cataloging process. Cataloging within ANCS+ is structured so that a collection-level record can be entered within the Collections Management Module, and additional refinement of the collection accomplished in the Archives Module. This refinement of information entails the description of collections in progressively finer units of detail, and should occur in consultation with a trained archivist.

The first level after the collection level is the series level; for example, this would be all files with a K code in a park's central files record collection. The next (third) level of description is the sub-series level, which following the same analogy, would be all D62 files. The fourth level of description is the file unit level, such as the D6226 file for FY1989. The last, and finest, level of description is at the item level, such as an individual piece of correspondence.

For another example, the entire contents of the map cases would be the park's maps and plans collection. Its series arrangement could be established based upon park structure or location (as is currently the case at AMME). The file level would be each set of plans for a project (a project could be at the sub- series level if it involved a main structure, a parking lot, and other sections of a construction project).

Some collections may be amply described at the series and then file unit level, thus providing the level of access needed by researchers but limiting the expenditure of time on description (by eliminating the sub-series and item level descriptions).

Occasionally, staff may determine that access by correspondent or person is not as great a priority as having access points provided reflecting a park's unique structure or organization. However, for donated manuscript collections, the persons writing, receiving, and being discussed in the manuscripts are of the utmost importance.

Physical Safety of Archives

As previously noted, AMME and WAPA have high inherent risks for natural disasters and environmental degradation. For park archival materials, duplication of information and off-island storage of duplicates is probably the best method for preserving information. Duplication and off-site storage is also appropriate for the park's digital records. A systematic planned approach should be used with the most likely-achievable and highest-value items scheduled for first reproduction and off-site storage.

Digital files can easily be copied onto external hard-drives, checked for fidelity, and then sent to a partner storage facility. Paper records will be handled similarly but require more effort. The NPS has a number of centers such as Harpers Ferry, Western Archeological Conservation Center, Technical Information Center, and WASO-NRID which offer off-site storage services for specialized information types. For the historic museum archival materials, like those found in rolled storage, duplication is only a partial solution and increased vigilance protecting the original is required. This concern with the original is because the original is also an artifact and not merely a tablet of information.

Training

WAPA has a number of new employees with little familiarity to NPS records and archival management. The administrative officer maintains central files but these are not fully used by other divisions. It is clear staff does not yet understand employee responsibility towards records and archival management.

In contrast with records management, museum archival management has a number of peculiarities that require the curator or museum technician to have an in-depth knowledge so as not to make existing circumstances worse. Additionally, some archival management activities are outside the purview of casually-educated staff and should be accomplished by a trained specialist.

Records management must be done by all employees. Offices that interact should coordinate records management to ensure adequate documentation is preserved. Training is an ongoing process and should be multi-faceted. Considering the isolation of Guam, a number of low cost training items can be instituted quickly and easily. The course recommendations given below focus primarily on records management, since this is what most of the park staff will be doing. As records of particular value to the park are then transferred into the museum archives, the curator and museum technician need further education. Lastly, as some of the park-wide decisions that are recommended are addressed, less repetitive training will be needed with existing staff.

NPS Records Management Training

All NPS employees must complete the 2008 Records Awareness and 2008 Orientation to Privacy courses. A Learning Plan has been developed in DOI LEARN to assign the courses to all NPS employees, contractors, partners, and volunteers. The learning plan has been assigned to all DOI LEARN accounts and monthly updates will occur thereafter for new accounts.

Records Management for Everyone: An Online Training Course for all Federal Employees. Find this at:

http://nara.learn.com/recordsmanagement-training

Records Management for Everyone provides an understanding of basic records management principles and how they affect daily work. This course explores the techniques and protocols that govern the lifecycle of a record, including concepts of adequate and proper documentation, disposition, and where to go for help. It discusses how managing records and information supports the work of the Federal government and improves staff effectiveness. There are no formal prerequisites.

By the end of this course, participants will be able to identify Federal records and the key requirements for managing them; understand records management principles; understand the repercussions of poor records management; and know where to go for records management assistance within an agency.

NPS Documents
Avoiding the Looming Black Hole: Managing Electronic Records for Now and for the Future (TEL Class) (doc) A new class focusing on the management of NPS electronic records.
https://ea.nps.gov/WhaleComFAD30877CCF6350A6864049C79272096C
BA4E8C0E1/WhaleCom0/documents/TEL%20Class%20Announcement
%20%286-07%29.doc

PowerPoint Slides from "Avoiding the Looming Black Hole..." Slides used in TEL class offered June 12, 2007.
https://ea.nps.gov/WhaleComFAD30877CCF6350A6864049C79272096C BA4E8C0E1/WhaleCom0/documents/Avoiding_the_Looming_Black_Hol e_Slides.ppt

Digital Migration Strategy

Digital preservation encompasses activities designed to extend the usable life of computer files and protect them from media failure, physical loss, and obsolescence. WAPA and AMME have invested a significant amount of time creating digital images that have long term value to the park. Photographic images, CAD (computer aided drafting) files, and scanned images compose the majority of digital files found onsite. Additional computer data is anticipated as new natural resource projects are started with cooperating agencies. In particular, water quality data and weather data will be added to the park inventory. The park should plan for the management of these digital resources into the future. For background information please consult with the Digital Preservation Management web site at http://www.icpsr.umich.edu/dpm/dpm-eng/introduction.html

For WAPA and AMME to use information proficiently and efficiently, a comprehensive, cross division strategy will have to be initiated in the park. The strategy will include linking divisional decision-making, adopting park policies, and encouraging continued staff efforts. Simultaneous with these efforts, the curator will have to bring existing resources into an arrangement that is cohesive and complimentary with all the plans and professional standards.

Storage Recommendations

Photographs: For black and white photographic film materials a stable, low non-varying relative humidity is much more important than a stable, low temperature. Refer to *Conserve O Gram* 14/4 "Caring for Photographs: General Guidelines," and 14/2 "Storage Enclosure for Photographic Prints and Negatives."

Figure 5 Photo donated by Bill Long, who served in Saipan during WWII, AMME – 0005

Digital Images: The NPS recommends using TIFF files for master digital files of digitized records. Master file formats should be housed off-line in uncompressed and non-proprietary formats. If master files must be compressed, lossless compression formats should be used. A data migration plan must be implemented so that data is copied and moved to the next generation of software and hardware each time any element of the system changes or when the files are older than five years. All files should be checked for fidelity when backed up onto an external drive.

Large Format Maps and Drawings: Storage enclosures for oversized materials depend upon the type of process that created each specific item in question. Types of processes noted at the park include bluelines (a type of diazotype), tracing paper, plain paper, aerial photographs, and Mylar™.

Existing recommendations for plain paper, aerial photographs, and blueprints are found in *Conserve O Gram* 19/16 "Housing Archival Paper-Based Materials." Plain paper and tracing papers, particularly the latter, can be acidic, so pH neutral, buffered folders are recommended. Blueprints (and cyanotypes) also require a pH neutral, unbuffered folder stock, as they are the result of an acidic developing process.

The recommended storage procedure among architectural maps and plans is a neutral pH, unbuffered, high-alpha cellulose, lignin-free board folder, with ten sheets or less per folder, interleaved with a neutral pH separation sheet.

Bluelines/diazotypes are very detrimental to all other objects. The result of an alkaline developing process, they are self-destructing from "inherent vice." They off-gas phenols and alkaline products such as ammonia. and they may contain and off-gas thiourea, a chemical very damaging to silver (photographic) processed images. These need to be isolated not only in folders, but also in separate drawers, away from all other maps, plans, and especially aerial photographs.

Park staff may also wish to interleave diazotypes for further chemical absorption. For the long-term preservation of information on diazotypes, duplication on chronoflex Mylar is recommended, or at a minimum, duplication onto high quality buffered paper. The diazotypes may then be used as copies or completely disposed of because of problems caused by their chemical off-gassing.

Oral Histories: The park has a number of oral histories in various formats and locations that should be managed as a collection in the museum archives. Additionally, the source tapes are old and require a format migration. Most oral interviews are cassette, VHS, or Hi-8 tapes. See below for specific material type storage recommendations for these types of items. Additionally, no paper transcripts exist for any of the interviews. Standard practice is to transcribe recordings and then edit the transcription and allow the interviewee to review the material.

Reports: Reports should be included in the associated project files and kept in the museum archival collection. The park should consider keeping a copy available in the library for park staff. However, copies of all park-generated reports should be sent to the Technical Information Center. TIC will scan, microfilm, and make the reports digitally available to NPS staff only, free of charge. The table below is a list of example items already on file at TIC for WAPA.

WAPA	Environmental Assessment - Construction Of An Interpretive Facility, Nimitz Hill, Asian Inland Unit With Finding Of No Significant Impact (FONSI)	Document	D26		9/1/1993	pub
WAPA	Preliminary Geotechnical Engineering Report - Asan Bay Overlook	Document	D27		11/15/1993	res
WAPA	Park & Recreation Areas-Territory Of Guam	Document	D28		1/1/1952	res
WAPA	The War In Micronesia - A Briefing Paper Prepared For The U. S. Park Service Of Guam	Document	D29		2/1/1980	pub
WAPA	EA/GMP	Document	D3		8/1/1981	pub
WAPA	Ea/Gimp	Document	D3	A	3/1/1983	pub
WAPA	Resource Management Plan	Document	D30		2/14/1997	res
WAPA	Strategic Plan And Annual Performance Plan	Document	D31		9/1/1997	res
WAPA	Stabilization Of Concrete Military Structures - Phase I: Investigation, Testing, And Documentation	Document	D32		8/20/1990	res
WAPA	New Area Master Plan - Proposed Guam National Seashore	Document	D33	A	2/6/1968	pub
WAPA	New Area Master Plan-Guam Ns	Document	D33		7/1/1967	res

Table 2 WAPA documents at the Technical Information Center, 2007

Film: Original motion picture film should be stored on archival film cores, rather than on reels, and in permanent and durable film boxes. The American Film Institute (AFI) in Los Angeles maintains a national database directory of motion picture films called the National Moving Image Database (NAMID). Contact AFI or the American Moving Image Association (AMIA) if park staff are uncertain if the park holds the last copy of an important historic film.

The following information should be recorded for motion picture film: location, reel sequence in the film, date process, emulsion type, generation and polarity (original negative, inter negative, soundtrack, projection print, etc.), color or black and white, sound or silent, gauge (8, 16, 35 or 70 mm), playback equipment necessary, soundtrack, creators (e.g., director and producer), title, subject, actors, and copyright information.

Audio and VHS Tapes (Oral History): magnetic media (VHS, Hi-8, audiocassette, reel-to-reel, and computer tapes) Virtually all of the magnetic tape older than as little as 10 years may be in serious jeopardy from deterioration.

Vertical etha-foam supports are recommended every six inches. Use etha-foam to insulate the metal drawers from the tapes. All magnetic media should be kept away from heat, light, ultraviolet radiation, and magnetic fields, including electric motors, and audio speakers. Tape media should be stored in the "as played" condition to maintain constant, even pressure on the tape (so that the tape is not stressed causing it to break). Gloves should be worn when handling all magnetic media, as the oils from skin leave a residue that can coat the playing heads of equipment and attract dust.

Recommended environmental conditions for long-term archival storage are between 25% and 45% relative humidity, and cold storage at 49° to 59°F, with a set point of 54°F and 40%, ±3% fluctuation maximum over a month's time.

Data that should be listed for audiocassette and reel-to-reel tapes includes: recording title and series, artist, composer, speaker, interviewer, interviewee or informant's name(s); biographies of interviewees or informants; recording date; number of cassettes in this title; broadcast date; subject matter; publication information (e.g., place, publisher, date, edition); whether an original or a copy; restrictions; playing speed; playing time; recording format and media; any special signal processing used (e.g., Dolby C); physical dimensions; existence of a script or transcript; and existence of a preservation duplicate copy and the copy's format.

Slides: Slides are a positive image on clear film. As with all photographic films, a low, constant relative humidity level is essential for the long-term preservation of this media. Please see *Conserve O Gram* 14/4, "Caring for Photographs: General Guidelines," which recommends storage conditions of 68°F or less and 20-30% relative humidity, with variation of less than 2° and 3%.

Recommendations

- Conduct a records survey using a professional archivist, make appropriate arrangement schemes, and consolidate approved files to the museum collection storage.

- Create or adopt a filing scheme in consultation with a trained archivist and with division level input. The policy should be disseminated to all park staff on yearly intervals and placed in the park orientation folder.

- Adopt an electronic records migration plan for existing park digital resources. The parks' digital image files (jpg, tiffs) and CAD files are of particular note.

- Include the curator in planning processes that have archival or museum management implications, such as the I&M research design or rehabilitating the Piti guns. Contact the I & M Network for a data management plan to ensure that protocol decisions are adequately documented and preserved.

- Consolidate archival material to the museum storage facility at the WAPA visitor center. It is the best location offering security, environmental control, and resource access for WAPA and AMME archives.

- Duplicate paper-based materials and distribute the copies to geographic areas with different risk profiles as a planned, prioritized effort in risk mitigation.

- Purchase five-drawer flat map cases (three initially) for proper storage of maps and drawings. Place cases near open files in museum storage with other map cases moved from the Administration offices.

- Contact Technical Information Center (TIC) to initiate a microfilm/scanning project of large format maps and drawings. TIC will microfilm/scan up to 500 sheets per month free of charge. Ask to have the originals returned to the park and only send items not already at TIC.

- Send to TIC all park-generated reports for scanning and microfilming. These should be copies, but originals can be sent if not book-bound. There is no charge for this service.

- Purchase polypropylene or similar records storage boxes, 50 large-size map folders (close to case drawer size), and two or three high-capacity external hard drives for copying electronic files which can then be stored off-island.

- Transcribe oral history tapes and create digital copies. Place a copy of known releases in accession files. Attempt to get releases missing from interviews.

- Arrange additional training for park staff in archival processing, re-housing, and describing. Contact a trained professional from outside the park with some historical knowledge of the resources.

- Set up an on-site visit with a trained professional archivist/records manager familiar with NPS museum policies to give staff solid records management training. PWR Records Manager Susan Ewing Haley, PORE Archivist Carolla DeRooy, or WASO-MMP Senior Archivist John W. Roberts could be contacted.

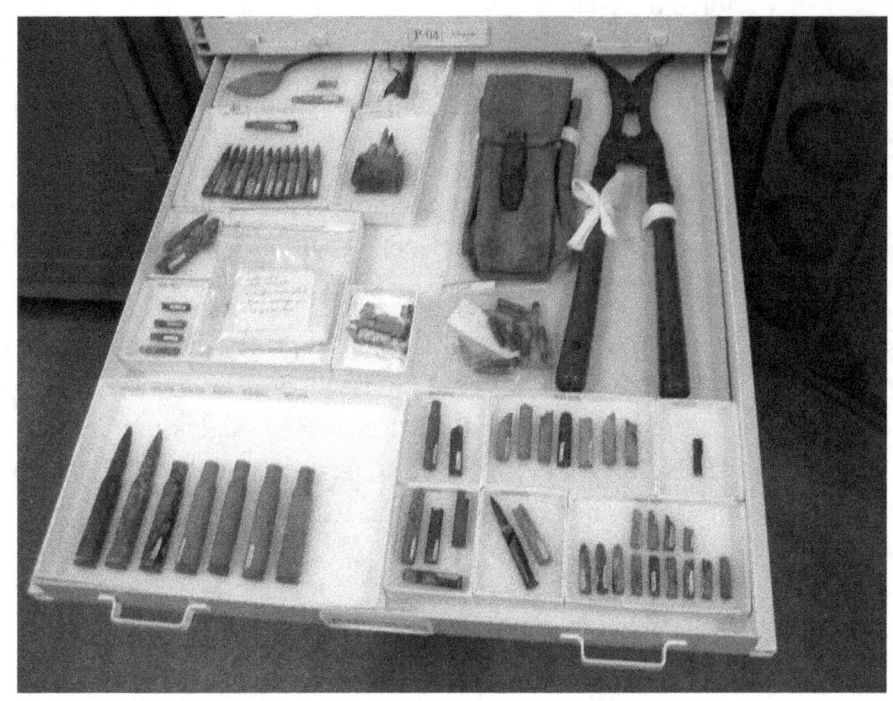

Figure 6 Storage drawer at WAPA

Figure 7 Japanese midget submarine

War in the Pacific NHP / American Memorial Park Museum Management Plan

Issue C —
Museum Development

Issue Statement:

An effective museum program requires professionalism, commitment, thorough documentation, and meaningful dialog with park staff, the public, partners, and stakeholders.

Background

War in the Pacific National Historical Park and American Memorial Park both possess important cultural resources pertaining to the Pacific Theater of the Second World War. An intrinsic, vital component of both parks' resources base is the two museum collections. Moderate in size by Servicewide standards, these collections are nonetheless highly significant respective to both American and world history. These tangible reminders allow one to experience vital personal linkages with both tragedy and triumph. World War II was the most destructive war in the planet's history, and yet it also has been called "The Good War," as the fall of fascism helped to usher in a new era of expanded democracy as well as the beginning of the end of colonialism. The various artifacts, papers, and photographs that are included with the two parks' collections, along with the battle sites and associated memorials in the parks provide an incomparable window into that long-ago era.

Items related to WWII in the Marianas Campaign and the entire Pacific Theater are the main components of the collection. And yet, the collections also, quite naturally, include natural history specimens documenting the two parks' biological diversity, as well as various archival collections related to resources management, construction, and maintenance activities.

Based on data in the 2007 WAPA Collection Management Report (CMR), the museum collection consists of 11,271 artifacts, specimens, and archival materials related to the park's themes, as well as to its cultural and natural history (see Table 3 below).

Discipline	Cataloged	Not Cataloged	Totals
Archeology	403	110	513
Ethnology	8	0	8
History	5,315	156	5,471
Archives	4,481	2	4,483
Biology	796	0	796
Paleontology	0	0	0
Geology	0	0	0
Totals	**11,003**	**268**	**11,271**

Table 3   WAPA museum collection data from the 2007 Collection Management Report

The museum collection at AMME is composed of 581 artifacts related to the park's theme, the WWII Marianas Campaign and the battles on Saipan. The park's 2007 Collection Management Report (Table 4 below) quantifies these collections by category.

Discipline	Cataloged	Not Cataloged	Totals
Archeology	41	0	41
Ethnology	0	0	0
History	460	80	540
Archives	0	0	0
Biology	0	0	0
Paleontology	0	0	0
Geology	0	0	0
Totals	**501**	**80**	**581**

Table 4   AMME museum collection data from the 2007 Collection Management Report

Museum collections are located in two structures: the AMME Visitor Center features exhibits only and the WAPA Visitor Center houses exhibits and serves as both collections' storage facility. As noted elsewhere in this document, these two new facilities provide state-of-the-art protection for these irreplaceable resources, while at the same time, the park staff is highly motivated, energetic, and enthusiastic in carrying out their stewardship responsibilities. The park staff is to be applauded for their dedication and for the tremendous progress that has been carried out since super-typhoon Pongsona destroyed the park's visitor center and collections facility in December 2002.

Discussion

Museum collections record the resources that the park is required to protect. They offer essential information for management decisions, serve as a unique resource for scientific investigators studying the natural and cultural processes that created the lands within the park, and assist interpretive staff in relating information to visitors. Documenting museum collections is essential; it allows both physical and intellectual access to museum collections for management, education, research, and loans.

Scope of Collection

The building block upon which a unit's museum collection is developed is the Scope of Collection Statement (SOCS). Similar to an acquisitions policy, the SOCS details what the park will collect for its museum collection and why, and yet the document is much more than simply an acquisitions policy. A Scope of Collection Statement is a stand-alone museum planning document that succinctly defines the scope of the unit's museum collection holdings at the present and for the future. The SOCS derives from the legislation establishing the unit, its mission, and its laws and regulations mandating the preservation of collections. The Scope of Collection Statement is the critical basis for managing museum collections.

The WAPA and AMME Scope of Collection Statements are in need of revision and update. Both documents were developed a number of years ago and do not fully address the two parks' legislative mandates, themes, and management objectives—nor do they address more recent developments pertaining to each park's evolving missions, goals, and partnerships. The parks have recognized the importance of update both SOCS, and are to be commended for their recent planning efforts relative to addressing this vital issue.

Development of a park's Scope of Collection Statement is one of the most important projects that the museum staff can undertake—the SOCS sets the tone for the direction that the collection will take. It provides guidance relative to the acquisition and management of those museum objects that contribute directly to the unit's mission, as well as those additional collections that the Service is legally mandated to preserve. The Scope of Collection Statement will:

- define the purpose of the museum collection;

- set agreed-upon limits that specify the subject matter, geographical location, and time period to which the collection must relate;

- evolve from legislation and planning documents specific to each unit, and from laws, regulations, and NPS policies governing research and specimen collection conducted within park boundaries;

- state what types of objects will be acquired to fulfill the park's mission; and

- consider collection use and restrictions.

Development of a Scope of Collection Statement is a group effort. For the document to be effective, the participation of the major collections generators and users is required. Though the curator will undoubtedly take the lead in preparing the SOCS, at a minimum, input from the resource management and interpretive staffs is necessary for an effective document.

Once the SOCS is approved by the superintendent, the curator can produce briefing statements for distribution to park staff, partners, stakeholders, and the public. These detail the park's scope of collection, specify the object types and quantities needed for the collection to be relevant to the park's mission, and offer a brief explanation as to why certain items are not required. The briefing statement intended for the public should also include information concerning other known institutions' collecting emphasis and contact information, in order to facilitate potential donations of items not needed by the NPS.

SOCS Revision: Acquisitions, Deaccessions, and Other Needed Adjustments

A review of the parks' current SOCS, existing museum collection holdings, enabling legislation, interpretive themes, resources management goals and objectives, and other issues of pertinence, readily shows that a number of additions, revisions, and updates are required of each SOCS.

The following list quantifies a number of specific related recommendations.

Needed Acquisitions

Neither park collection includes objects of material culture related to the Mariana Islands' indigenous peoples; the Chamorros and Carolinians. The missions of both the Guam Museum and the Commonwealth of the Northern Mariana Islands Museum of History and Culture (CNMI Museum) are devoted to interpreting and preserving the complete history of the islands, especially that of the Chamorro and Carolinian cultures.

Although the parks do not intend to duplicate these two museums' collections, there is nonetheless a need for the WAPA and AMME collections to include a small number of such items, primarily Chamorro and Carolinian ethnographic and historic materials dating from both pre-WWII and the wartime periods. Such collections can help to provide context—what were the imperialistic aims of both the United States and Japan related to the Marianas Islands and other areas of the Pacific and East Asia, and why did the two nations eventually embark upon war?

AMME is extremely grateful to the CNMI Museum for its generosity in allowing the park to exhibit a number of items from its collection (pre-war and internment camp objects) in the AMME Visitor Center. However, the park desires to obtain a limited number of similar objects for inclusion in its permanent collection in the near future.

Although Japanese arms (firearms and edged weaponry) are well represented within the two parks' collections, there is a dearth of American and Allied weapons. The collection lacks uniforms, equipment, personal property, papers, archives, and other associated collections related to the Allies and other armed forces resisting the Japanese Empire in the Pacific Theater (Australia, New Zealand, Republic of China, Chinese Communist forces, Soviet Union, as well as guerillas and nationalist movements in the Philippines, French Indochina, Dutch East Indies, and other occupied lands).

Potential Deaccessions

During the upcoming SOCS review and revision, it is essential (as noted above) to include park natural resources management personnel throughout the process. Natural resources management project documentation (archives) should be included in the museum collection but what specimen types should be included to best serve the park's research needs? Are extensive voucher collections required, or do other area institutions' collections (such as University of Guam, U.S. Fish and Wildlife Service) meet these needs? Are physical specimens required or are data (including photographs and recordings) sufficient? When an approved research project generates specimens to be retained, is the park or an outside repository the most suitable curation facility? By including park natural resources management staff in the SOCS process from the beginning, the final document will also reflect the needs of the park relative to science, research, and management of natural resources.

Currently, the WAPA natural science collection includes the herbarium, two *Tridacna gigas* (giant clam) specimens, and two endangered sea turtle specimens. The sea turtles, *Chelonia mydas* (green sea turtle) and *Eretmochelys imbricata* (hawksbill sea turtle), were seized by special agents from the National Oceanic and Atmospheric Administration (NOAA). These specimens, on long-term loan to the park from NOAA, were officially transferred to the NPS in 2007. The park may want to discuss the permanent disposition of these specimens, in particular:

- Are the specimens of such importance for research and/or interpretive purposes that they should remain in the park's collection? If so, should one or both be on exhibit, in storage, or a combination? If the specimens are to be retained, the appropriate permits should be obtained from NOAA's National Marine Fisheries Service.

- If the giant clam specimens are judged to be unnecessary for the research and interpretive needs of the park, they should be deaccessioned. Perhaps the Guam National Wildlife Refuge (U.S. Fish and Wildlife Service), the University of Guam, Guam Museum, CNMI Museum, or another governmental, educational, or other non-profit public institution could provide a suitable home for the specimens.

Items in Need of Deaccession

The WAPA collection includes a limited number of items that are suitable for deaccession. These items consist of:

- **Oversized Objects:** These include the Japanese guns at Ga'an Point, torpedo at Asan Beach, and the mines located at the maintenance yard. All of these objects should be deaccessioned, with disposition as follows:

  - Ga'an Point Guns: Deaccession and include on the park's List of Classified Structures (LCS).

  - Asan Beach Torpedo: Deaccession and include on the park's List of Classified Structures (LCS).

- **Naval Mines:** Deaccession and attempt to find a suitable home with another museum (contact the WASO Museum Clearinghouse for assistance).

- **WWII Homefront Materials:** The collection includes a number of items related to the WWII homefront and/or the European Theater. These items should be deaccessioned and transferred to appropriate NPS units on the mainland, such as Rosie the Riveter or Golden Gate. If not needed by other parks, the WASO Museum Clearinghouse can assist in placing these items with an appropriate institution.

- **Postwar Items:** Other items in the collection date after WWII. One such example is a War Bond poster from the Korean War. Such objects should be deaccessioned and transferred to appropriate museums with the assistance of the WASO Museum Clearinghouse.

Museum Documentation

Once the Scope of Collection Statement is approved and collections are acquired, all related museum documentation must meet NPS museum standards. Accession and catalog records must be accurate, legible, and unambiguous. The accession records describe the movement of items to and from the collection and document their legal status. The catalog records provide descriptive and location information for museum objects and specimens. These records provide valuable information that identifies the unique and irreplaceable resources associated with the park. Without accurate documentation, this information will be lost. Documentation is a major part of the accountability process for museum collection management. Correspondingly, accurate documentation also is vital for the collection's use for research and educational purposes. Without complete and accurate descriptions, provenance, and other catalog data which quantifies its unique characteristics, an item's potential for research or interpretive use is severely diminished, if not eliminated.

Museum documentation is not an issue at either WAPA or AMME—the museum staff is extremely conscientious in carrying out its mandated charges in this regard. All museum collections are accessioned, cataloged, stored, maintained, and exhibited (including an extensive online exhibition) in accordance with accepted museum standards and NPS requirements as noted in the *Museum Handbook*. The park is to be commended for the excellence of its museum documentation efforts, a vital component of its equally impressive overall collections management program.

When assessing a collections management program of such high caliber as that of WAPA and AMME, the majority of recommendations to be offered the park by the MMP team are relatively minor fine-tuning. These include:

- Rebind the WAPA accession book. Before the accession book leaves the park for rebinding, it should be photocopied in its entirety.

- Remove Post-It® notes from the accession book and accession files.

- Erase pencil notations in the accession book. If information is important enough to remain in the accession book, it should be written in permanent ink.

- Prepare permanent labels for the herbarium folders in the WAPA herbarium collection.

- Work with the chief of Interpretation to transfer oral history release forms and other documentation to the park archives.

- Determine if the oral history collection delivered to the park by University of Guam staff in 2007 (students' projects) is appropriate for the archival collection. If not, return to the university.

- Consult with the Department of History, University of Guam, to ascertain and resolve ownership, copyright, and use issues (including release permissions from interviewees) for the oral history collection delivered to the park by university staff in 2007, if appropriate for the WAPA collection:

- Photocopies of both the AMME and WAPA accession books should be maintained off-site to safeguard this information in the event of a major disaster. One copy could be housed within an insulated fire-resistant filing cabinet (UL®-listed 1-Hour Class 350 Fire with Impact) at WAPA headquarters. A second copy could be housed in a similar manner at another NPS unit, perhaps the USS Arizona Memorial.

- Electronic backup copies of the park's ANCS+ database should be similarly protected in the event of a catastrophic event. Backup data should be housed in a media vault, minimum UL® Class 125 1-Hour Fire Rating. One set of data should be so secured at WAPA headquarters and another set at a separate NPS unit.

Museum Planning

The park has already implemented a number of the various museum planning documents mandated by NPS *Management Policies*, *Director's Order #24: Museum Collections*, and *Director's Order #28: Cultural Resources Management*. Such documents can identify deficiencies, state recommended outcomes, and develop both interim and long-term action plans to accomplish these preferred end products. Examples include the Museum Security Survey, Museum Fire Protection Survey, Museum Collections Emergency Operations Plan (MEOP), and Museum Integrated Pest Management (IPM) Plan, all of which can be funded through the MCPPP program. Specific information pertaining to the various park planning documents related to the museum collection include:

- Scope of Collection Statement (SOCS) – there is no fund source available for this document. It is generally completed by park staff. See discussion above.

- Collection Condition Survey (CCS) – this is Museum Checklist standard H6. Based upon the assessment of the collection conducted during the MMP team site visit by the team conservator, a CCS is not needed at either park.

- Museum Emergency Operations Plan (MEOP) – Every park must have a MEOP, which should be a component of the park's overall Emergency Operations Plan. Museum Checklist standard E8 pertains to the MEOP. Preparation and implementation of a MEOP qualifies for MCPPP funding. The park is slated to receive funding for an MEOP (for both WAPA and AMME) in FY2009.

- Integrated Pest Management (IPM) Plan – this should be part of the parkwide IPM plan. Museum Checklist standard H8 pertains to the Museum IPM Plan. Preparation and implementation of a Museum IPM Plan qualifies for MCPPP funding and is a necessary first step in the development and implementation of an ongoing museum IPM program. A Museum IPM Plan for WAPA/AMME was funded in FY2008 and is currently in progress.

- Museum Preventive Maintenance Plan (called a Housekeeping Plan in the Museum Checklist) – This is Museum Checklist Standard H9. The WAPA Museum Preventive Maintenance Plan was completed early in FY2008. A similar plan should be prepared for the AMME Visitor Center; the park is encouraged to develop a PMIS project statement to address this need.

- Museum Security Survey and Museum Fire Protection Survey: neither WAPA nor AMME have implemented museum security surveys or museum fire protection surveys. The park is encouraged to develop PMIS project statements to address these needs. Park staff can work with the regional curator, regional structural fire management officer, and regional chief ranger to accomplish this work.

Fire and security surveys for all museum areas are critical requirements; these surveys identify needs and deficiencies and thereby establish the groundwork upon which these needs are to be addressed. These surveys can be funded through the MCPPP Program.

Staffing

As noted in the History of Collections section, the park has maintained a museum curator position for many years. During much of that time, the curator was within the Division of Interpretation. By January 2001, the curator reported directly to the superintendent, and in 2006, a separate Division of Cultural Resources Management was established. This new division, which is only two years old, consists of two employees comprising 1.5 FTE, allocated as follows:

Chief of Cultural Resources Management (Museum Curator, GS-1015-11), 1.0 FTE. The position description for the chief of CRM is the National Park Service Resources Careers Benchmark Position Description for a museum curator. This position description is very general in nature and provides no specific guidance on the extensive work for the two parks that the incumbent has carried out (and continues to accomplish) during her tenure. At some point the position description should be revised to include the specific work, especially program management duties, that the incumbent carries out.

Park Ranger (Park Ranger, Resource Protection, GS-025-05), 0.5 FTE. This part-time position is currently filled by a Student Career Experience Program (SCEP) employee/University of Guam student who works at WAPA 24 hours per week during the school year and 40 hours per week during the school breaks. The position is essentially a museum technician/park ranger, with approximately 80% of the duties composed of: accessioning, cataloging, and researching museum collections; environmental monitoring; museum recordkeeping and inventories; IPM monitoring; museum housekeeping; re-housing collections; and assisting the chief of CRM with various resource management projects, inventories, assessments, and so on. The remainder of the incumbent's time is devoted to interpretation (especially tours of the park for visiting veterans groups, military officers and spouses, and other VIPs) and other duties as assigned. This position is partially funded by project accounts.

A tremendous amount of good work has been accomplished, and the CRM staff is to be heartily congratulated. Over the past few years and continuing today, the division has performed (and still performs) miracles. It has:

- reestablished the museum program following the disastrous December 2002 super-typhoon Pongsona, which destroyed the park's visitor center and collections facility;

- moved into a new collections storage facility and completed a total re-housing project for the collection;

- (is) installing a new permanent exhibition in the new visitor center;

- helped measure for mounts and installed the artifacts into the Insular Guard Case and is in the process of helping select and design permanent exhibits;

- eliminated virtually all of its identified catalog backlog;

- implemented or is currently preparing a number of important museum planning documents;

- digitized a large component of its museum collection holdings in order to provide enhanced public access, especially for individuals who may be unable to visit the park; and

- developed (and continues to organize and mount) numerous online exhibitions featuring objects and photographs from the parks' museum collections, archival materials from other institutions' collections (National Archives and various park partners), as well as linkages to other websites of interest to park visitors, researchers, and students of WWII in the Pacific Theater.

Figure 8 Exhibit case at AMME

As a result of this extensive list of accomplishments, coupled with the transfer of the Japanese midget submarine from the Navy and the preservation needs of the various guns and other large outdoor objects, it became readily apparent during the MMP team site visit that the division's long-term staffing plan will require a minor modification: conversion of the GS-025-05 Park Ranger position to a GS-1010-09/11 Exhibit Specialist.

Exhibit Specialist

This position would be responsible for carrying out the bulk of the day-to-day preservation duties at the park. It could be classified as a museum technician with additional preventive maintenance duties relative to monuments, features, and sites. However, because so much has already been accomplished in the museum, and the outdoor exhibits appear to be the highest priority for the program in the foreseeable future, the exhibit specialist series appears to be more suitable for this work. The Final Report WAPA & AMME Organization and Review Operations document does not include any positions in Cultural Resources besides the current Museum Curator; this position would, however, provide for direct preservation and protection of park resources.

The position should be recruited at the GS-09/11 level, in order to appeal to a large, diverse pool of applicants. This would allow for the position to be filled as either a training position or at the full performance level if candidates who already possess such skills and experience apply. The primary duties of the exhibit specialist would include:

- documentation, stabilization, and preventive maintenance activities (supervising and/or carrying out) on the Japanese midget submarine, Ga'an Point guns, Piti guns, Asan Overlook Memorial, bunkers, fortifications, and other cultural features within the two parks;

- conducting preventive maintenance training for park maintenance staff (as they can assist with periodic preventive maintenance duties for guns, memorials, and sites);

- accessioning, cataloging, researching, exhibiting, and storing museum collections;

- museum recordkeeping, collections inventories, and annual reporting;

- museum housekeeping, including environmental monitoring and integrated pest management;

- planning, design, and installation of temporary museum exhibits; and

- assisting the chief of CRM with various resource management projects, inventories, assessments, and so on.

Communication and Partnerships

Communicating the responsibilities and benefits of the museum program to the park staff is essential. The ability of all divisions to work together as a team can be a major force in accomplishing the long-term goals of the park. The role of the museum program in this team effort spans the lifetime of each project. As projects are developed, the museum archives and collections can provide historical background. At the implementation stage, museum staff input ensures that data generated by the project is collected thoroughly and in a format that is compatible with archival and museum storage. As projects are completed, the museum provides a safe, accessible, and permanent repository for the final project data, artifacts, and/or specimens. This comprehensive collection of information is then available for use in the future for further projects.

The training of staff in proper records management has been discussed earlier in this section and in Issue B. Development of standard practices within each division of the park in consultation with the museum staff will facilitate the orderly flow of materials into the archives and museum collection. It is then the responsibility of the museum staff to facilitate access to the collection for entire park team.

The NPS Inventory and Monitoring program has completed their literature search for natural resources records related to the parks. These valuable records are now available to WAPA and AMME for resource management purposes. The natural resource division creates special challenges in the records management area because of the nature of its projects. Many projects will span several years and/or be led by outside investigators. It is the responsibility of the museum staff to review research proposals in light of compliance issues as well as data recovery. Having a strong system of data management in place before projects are initiated is essential.

The NPS Research Permit and Reporting System is an excellent tool for organizing the projects of this division. Permits for park-generated projects as well as those led by outside principle investigators establish an automatic filing system, yearly reporting system and a set of regulations which require data, reports, and publications generated from these studies to be provided to the park. The use of the museum catalog database to generate templates for the collection of specimen data ensures that specimens are accompanied by appropriate data and that the data is in a format that is readily transferable to the museum collection. The resulting information in the museum catalog, archives, and library can be a valuable tool for the natural resource staff. An attempt should be made to retrieve data, reports, publications, and any specimen information from previous projects conducted within the park.

Communication and cooperation with entities outside the parks has assisted both parks in their interpretive mission. The cultural resource manager has worked extensively with Francis X. Hezel SJ of the Micronesia Seminar, a research institute on Pohnpei and the Guam Humanities Council. Future collaboration with these agencies is anticipated. Approximately 2000 images are now available online as a result of these partnerships, with additional work at the National Archives and the uploading of cataloged photos and artifacts. The ability to display materials on the web can be crucial to collections acquisition. A case in point is that of George Tweed, the famous U.S. Navy radioman who evaded capture by the Japanese on Guam during the war years, with the assistance of the local Chamorro population. His daughter, Lolly Tweed, was interested in donating some of his war-time possessions but was reluctant to do so because the park could not promise to exhibit them in the museum. The possibility of having the items on permanent display on the web was the deciding factor in her decision to proceed with the donation.

Other NPS parks which might have Pacific Theater artifacts (such as USS Arizona Memorial, Rosie the Riveter, and Golden Gate) should be contacted for potential loans, transfers, or exchanges. Parks in the Service could also direct potential donors to WAPA and AMME.

Collections have been loaned to WAPA from the Guam Museum in the past. The Guam Museum, another victim of super-typhoon Pongsona, is in the process of building a new museum building. Members of the WAPA staff have been involved in the development of the museum plans. Strengthening the relationship between WAPA and the Guam Museum could assist both agencies. WAPA is in need of ethnography materials related to the Mariana Islands' indigenous peoples for interpretation and the Guam Museum is trying to raise awareness and money for their new facility. A loan of select materials from the Guam Museum collection to WAPA could be used to develop an interpretive display at WAPA. The selected items would also be maintained in a safe environment for the duration of the loan.

The close relationship between the park and the Guam Museum could facilitate directing public donations to the appropriate museum and allow for further collaboration. WAPA should also offer curatorial assistance to the Guam Museum staff and include them in NPS training opportunities. The offer of curatorial assistance may be appreciated at this time as the Guam Museum collection is housed under less than ideal conditions while awaiting its new facility.

The Commonwealth of the Northern Marianas Islands Museum of History and Culture (CNMI Museum) loaned items to AMME for the AMME Visitor Center exhibits but these objects were recently removed from exhibit and returned to the CNMI due to the exorbitant power bills for the AMME VC. A General Agreement is in place between AMME and the CNMI Museum for the purpose of reciprocal assistance in the event of an emergency. One of the goals of the partnership is for the CNMI Museum to focus on Mariana Islands history and ethnography, while AMME's collections are devoted to the military aspects of WWII in the Mariana Islands. Maintaining and strengthening this partnership can benefit both entities. Any exhibit on loan at AMME from the CNMI Museum should include information about the CNMI Museum, and CNMI Museum brochures should be available to visitors. The CNMI Museum should also be included in interpretive talks, providing another resource for visitors. This close relationship will also facilitate directing public donations to the appropriate museum. AMME might also offer curatorial assistance to the CNMI Museum staff and include them in NPS training opportunities.

The University of Guam provided for the care of the WAPA herbarium collection after super-typhoon Pongsona in December 2002. The University of Guam may also be a source of volunteer assistance to the museum program. Many universities include internship programs which require students to volunteer in the community doing work related to their discipline. It would be advantageous to the museum program to investigate this possibility. The ability of the volunteer to focus on one task to the exclusion of other museum work can lead to the efficient completion of otherwise overwhelming projects.

The U.S Navy is also an important and continuing partner at WAPA. The recent transfer of an extensive collection of artifacts and a midget Japanese submarine to the WAPA collection from the Navy creates new and exciting interpretive possibilities. WAPA's cooperation with the Navy extends to the park's visitor center being located in a U.S. Navy building on U.S. Navy property. There is great potential for enlisting Navy personnel, their spouses, or families as Volunteers in the Parks.

As the veterans of WWII and their families make decisions about the disposition of war-related materials, there will be many opportunities to expand the museum collection. However, the location of these national parks at such a distance from the mainland will necessitate an aggressive program to inform the public of the park's museum program and encourage them to donate related materials. The collection policies of the parks should be easily located on the parks' webpage along with information for potential donors. These donors could fill out an online form describing the objects and their history. The museum staff would then be able to decide which items are of interest.

Contacting the editors of widely-circulated periodicals and journals and explaining the mission of the parks and the need for collections may lead to articles about the parks or, at the very least, links to the website for potential donors.

Other museums which may also have materials relevant to the Pacific Theater should be contacted. These would include military museums managed by the U.S Army, Navy, Marine Corps, and Air Force, as well as all the Allied nations that participated in the Pacific Theater of World War II. In the case of international museums, both military and civilian institutions (especially national museums) should be contacted. Partnerships with these institutions might lead to transfers, exchanges, or loans of artifacts. If a potential donation to one of these museums in this new "Pacific War Museum Partnership" were not needed, a donor could be redirected to another partner whose scope of collection or acquisition needs are a more appropriate match. Another benefit of such a partnership would undoubtedly facilitate improved communications, loan, events, research, and other such cooperative endeavors in the public interest. Finally, each institution's website could be linked to that of every other partner institution.

Recommendations

- Revise Scope of Collection Statement for each park and broaden to include the entire Pacific Theater of WWII.

- Refrain from acquiring additional monumental objects following acquisition of the midget submarine.

- Broaden the SOCS to include ethnography materials from the Pacific Islands indigenous peoples.

- Develop a collections policy in consultation with natural resources for natural history specimen acquisition.

- Ensure that resource management records migrate to the archives in a timely manner.

- Note specific types of materials to be acquired in order to fulfill the mission of the parks.

- Revise current OFS statement 7374A or create a new statement for a GS-1010-09/11 Exhibit Specialist.

- Submit a PMIS statement for an archives survey.

- Submit a PMIS statement for records management training.

- Explore creating a partnership with the Guam Museum and extending the partnership with the Commonwealth of Mariana Islands Museum of History and Culture for exhibit interests and NPS training opportunities.

- Develop a standard donations information form for both parks which potential donors could use to describe their collection; make it available on the park website and at the front desk of each park.

- Develop site bulletins on the parks' museum collections, park preservation and protection efforts which promote donations (including what the park can accept) to the park.

- Explore setting up links to the WAPA and AMME websites from other WWII sites. Sites could include war-related NPS parks, other war-related museums and veterans' sites. Francis X. Hezel SJ may be an excellent source to suggest such institutions.

- Develop a "Pacific War Museum Partnership" with U.S. military museums (Army, Navy, Marine Corps, and Air Force), service museums in New Zealand, Australia, the Philippines, China, Japan, Russia, and other countries within the WWII Pacific Theater, and those countries' national museums. Such a partnership should facilitate transfers, exchanges, or loans of artifacts, joint exhibitions, improved communications, events, research, and other such cooperative endeavors in the public interest. Then link each institution's website to that of every other partner institution.

Figure 9 WAPA museum collections storage

Figure 10 Exhibit at AMME

Issue D —
Safety, Security, and Physical Facilities

Issue Statement

Public and staff safety, along with collections preservation, requires an investment in the planning, development, and maintenance of physical facilities and supporting action plans.

Background

The administratively-combined units of the American Memorial Park on Saipan and the War in the Pacific National Historical Park on Guam both contain museum collections. The collections facility at WAPA serves as the primary museum storage and records center for the combined units, whereas the collections at AMME are largely limited to materials on exhibit, and limited archival materials in the unit files. The WAPA building belongs to the Navy, and there is a five-year lease now in effect covering NPS occupancy of the structure.

The building at AMME is a recently designed and constructed visitor center with a small component for collections storage and work. The facility at WAPA is a former Army Reserve armory that has been renovated to serve as the park visitor center and a consolidated unit collections work and storage. Both structures appear to adequately fill the current needs of the two units, and to contain adequate space to serve the projected growth and development of the combined collections for the foreseeable future. Some limited facility concerns will be discussed later in this issue.

Regarding safety and physical security operational plans, both units have the elements of a Museum Collections Emergency Operations Plan (MCEOP) in place; however, these plans are dated (and out-of-date) because of staff changes at both parks, and neither has a cover sheet signed by the superintendent.

Both units also have written opening and closing procedures. The AMME procedures are dated 2005, and the WAPA procedures are undated. Neither set of procedures have a cover sheet signed by the superintendent.

The WAPA unit has a Collections Access Policy dated 2008; however, it does not have a cover sheet signed by the superintendent. Since the WAPA unit serves as the collections repository for the AMME collections, a separate access policy for the AMME collections is not needed.

AMME is covered under a General Agreement with the Northern Mariana Islands Museum of History and Culture concerning joint preservation and protection of museum collections in case of natural disaster (such as typhoons). This annual agreement was renewed this year and is in effect until September 2009.

WAPA currently has no law enforcement program. Memorials in the parks are routinely vandalized and, in one case, stolen for their metal resale value. While there are two Law Enforcement Rangers at AMME, this does not provide adequate cover for that park, let alone the many and frequent needs of WAPA.

Discussion

By virtue of having new or recently renovated structures housing collections, plus having adequate space for both storage and work space for the foreseeable future, these combined units are more fortunate than many of their counterparts. As a result, it will not be necessary to discuss serious building condition and maintenance problems that would be difficult and expensive to mitigate. A few minor safety problems will be discussed along with the continuing (and future) electrical power problems for both sites. A secondary issue of planning needs and issues will follow.

The MMP team noted two safety situations within the collections work and storage area of the WAPA facility. One was a difference of several inches in elevation between the collections area and the rest of the building. This had been mitigated by the installation of a concrete ramp connecting the two levels. Since the team's visit, however, a guard rail has been installed.

Also, the floor covering in the collections storage area is separating from the concrete floor in at least three locations, causing it to "bubble" and rise off the floor. The largest patch covers about three square feet and is about one inch in height. These bubbles are difficult to see because of the pattern and color of the floor covering, and could easily cause staff to trip, which in turn could lead to physical injury and/or the damage or destruction of museum property. Repair options need to be discussed with the firm responsible for installing the floor covering prior to warranty expiration.

There appear to be on-going compressor problems with the air conditioning systems at both visitor centers. Two compressors have been replaced at the AMME unit since it opened for operation less than two years ago. The air conditioning unit servicing the exhibit area at the WAPA visitor center makes a "squeal" when starting that could also be related to a compressor problem. Fitting the air conditioning compressors at both locations with electrostatic filters, and aggressively maintaining them, should increase the working life of the units at both visitor centers.

By far the most serious situation to face both facilities is the development of sustainable power sources. The Saipan power grid is supported by a diesel generator system that dates from the German occupation of the island prior to World War I, and spare parts for these generators need to be custom made. The electrical bill for the AMME facility is $18,000 per month ($8,000 actual power bill plus a $10,000 surcharge), which has led to a serious budgetary shortfall at this unit for the fiscal year.

The new visitor center was constructed for, and equipped with, a diesel generator capable of supporting the unit's electrical needs. This was originally done in response to the brown-outs and black-outs common to the Saipan power grid; the generator is equipped with an automatic system that starts the generator in case of power grid interruption. During the on-site visit the team was informed that the auto-start feature was not working properly. The park is considering the option of running that generator rather than continuing using electricity supplied by the Saipan power grid at the current rates.

The power grid on Guam is more dependable and also less expensive (about $2,900 per month for the visitor center operation). A standby generator was purchased for the visitor center during renovation, but the project lacked the funding to purchase and install the automatic system to start the generator in case of power grid interruption. The generator currently has no auto-start system. It will cost approximately $11,000 for the generator to turn on automatically in the event of a power outage. Funding should be sought to make this facility improvement as soon as possible.

Apparently the air conditioning systems at both visitor centers lacked a hot gas bypass system at installation. This system removes a percentage of the ambient humidity from the intake air prior to cooling, which in turn stabilizes the humidity within the building envelope. Dry air feels cooler than humid air, allowing the actual temperature levels for human comfort to be higher, and cooling costs to be lower.

The air conditioning controls at both visitor centers are currently the manual sliding type controls. These should be converted to digital thermostats as soon as possible. This will provide a more accurate control over the temperature in the different zones, resulting in a savings of power costs. Additionally, both park and association staff should be discouraged from changing preset temperature controls. The suggested addition of a hot gas bypass system to lower the ambient humidity will also help to discourage staff from changing thermostat settings.

The combined units of the park will be undergoing an energy audit during the summer of 2008, and this plan urgently suggests that the consideration of solar power for both units be seriously considered. These systems would be expensive to purchase, install, and maintain, but should significantly reduce dependence of the combined units upon the local power grids, as well as significantly reduce the parks' carbon footprint.

In addition to the work necessary to complete the visitor center physical facilities and make them as self sufficient and "green" as possible, additional administrative, planning, and procedural actions and documents are required for both units.

Chief among these is the need for a long-term lease between the National Park Service and the Navy to cover the recently renovated WAPA visitor center. While the negotiation and finalization of a long-term agreement is clearly beyond the brief and responsibility level of this Museum Management Plan team, it is suggested that resolution of this situation receive a high priority from both the park and regional specialists in these matters.

Both visitor centers would be well served by receiving a thorough Security and Fire Protection Survey. This survey would review the existing physical security and fire detection systems, and suggest necessary refinements and improvements. The Federal Protective Service will do these surveys for National Park Service units, often free of charge. The Navy might also be available to assist.

Since the park currently has very minimal law enforcement coverage, the need for a law enforcement program is vital to the parks' protection of natural and cultural resources. With the potential growth and development on Guam this will likely become a more critical issue there, but it is a continuing concern on Saipan as well.

The Museum Collections Emergency Operations Plan for each visitor center should be updated and provided with signed and dated cover sheets. Operational versions of these plans should be prepared in three-ring binder format, and located where staff may access them in each visitor center. In order to be fully effective, these plans need to be exercised on a regular basis.

Opening and Closing Procedures for each visitor center were recently updated but need superintendent approval. These procedures should also be prepared in three-ring binder format and located where staff may access them in each visitor center.

The existing Collections Access Policy should be provided with a signed and dated cover sheet, and made available to staff as needed.

The General Agreement between American Memorial Park and CNMI museum for joint preservation and protection of museum collections has been renegotiated and renewed for one year.

Recommendations

- Develop a "concerns list" specific to the security and preservation of museum collections in each visitor center in cooperation with the chief of Maintenance for the combined parks, and the lead maintenance worker for AMME.

- Use the "concerns list" as a basis to develop the work and project statements necessary to correct the identified problem areas.

- Work with the Maintenance Division to correct safety problems identified at the WAPA storage facility.

- Work with an HVAC engineer and the Maintenance Division to determine the appropriate and most energy efficient system needed for the preservation of museum collections and the comfort of staff and visitors. Once that is done, submit a PMIS statement for any funding needed to address the issue.

- Work with the region to develop an adequate law enforcement program that will ensure the protection of cultural and natural resources.

- Complete a security survey and a fire protection survey for both visitor centers, perhaps using the Federal Protective Services or comparable United States Navy security services.

- Develop an action plan for the improvement of security and fire systems and document the projected needs for funding upon receipt and review of written Security and Fire Protection reports.

- Revise and update the park-level procedural documents for collections access, opening and closing procedures, and emergency operations. Ensure the applicable portions of these documents are reviewed and approved by the superintendent, and are made available in useable format to park and association staff.

Bibliography

Good museum management planning requires an understanding of the library, archives, and museum collection resources as they currently exist, background on how and why these resources were developed, and information on what is required to preserve the resources and make them available for use. To be effective, planners must first review park-specific documentation such as reports, checklists, and plans, then make recommendations based on professional theory and techniques that are documented in the professional literature.

This bibliography lists the park-specific materials used in developing the War in the Pacific National Historical Park/American Memorial Park Museum Management Plan.

Duchesne, Tammy. *American Memorial Park Visitor Center Emergency Operation Procedures*. Hagåtña, GU: U.S. Department of the Interior, National Park Service, Pacific West Region, 2008.

Evans-Hatch and Associates, Inc. *War in the Pacific National Historical Park: An Administrative History*. Hagåtña, GU: U.S. Department of the Interior, National Park Service, Pacific West Region, 2004.

Floray, Steve. *War in the Pacific National Historical Park Museum Preservation Maintenance Plan*. Hagåtña, GU: U.S. Department of the Interior, National Park Service, Pacific West Region, 2008.

National Park Service, Pacific Islands System Support Office. *Resource Management Plan War in the Pacific National Historical Park*. Honolulu, HI: U. S. Department of the Interior, National Park Service, 1997.

National Park Service. *General Management Plan American Memorial Park Saipan Commonwealth of the Northern Mariana Islands*. San Francisco, CA: U.S. Department of the Interior, National Park Service, Western Regional Office, 1989.

National Park Service. *General Management Plan War in the Pacific National Historical Park Guam.* San Francisco, CA: U.S. Department of the Interior, National Park Service, Western Regional Office, 1983.

National Park Service. *Statement for Management War in the Pacific National Historical Park Guam.* Hagåtña, GU: U.S. Department of the Interior, National Park Service, Western Region, 1988.

National Park Service. *War in the Pacific National Historical Park/American Memorial Park Emergency Response Plan.* Hagåtña, GU: U.S. Department of the Interior, National Park Service, Pacific West Region, ND.

Thompson, Erwin N. *Historic Resource Study War in the Pacific National Historical Park Guam.* Denver, CO: U. S. Department of the Interior, National Park Service, 1985.

Appendix A —
Archiving Resource Management Field Records

The purpose of this Standard Operating Procedure (SOP) is to aid park staff in accomplishing their responsibilities according to *NPS-77 Natural Resources Management Guidelines, DO#28: Cultural Resources Management Guidelines, DM-411: DOI Property Management Regulations, DO#19: Records Management Guidelines, 36 CFR 2.9* and legislation associated with archiving resource management records.

The history of incorporating archival materials into the park museum collection is documented in the annual park Collection Management Report. In addition, the *NPS Museum Handbook,* Part II, Appendix D documents the need for guidelines for the management of archival material. Directions are included for the retention of report concerning both cultural and natural scientific research conducted within and for the park.

The park's archives include many unique information resources that need professional organization and arrangement to promote their most efficient use. Park resource management staff generates records on a daily basis that should be considered for inclusion in the park archives. Staff creates data sets, photographs, maps, and field notebooks that future generations will need to access to research the history of cultural and natural resource projects at the park.

Park staff is involved in capturing fire monitoring data, plant collections, air quality research, and a host of ethnographic and archeological research. Preserving the institutional knowledge of each of these individual activities depends ultimately upon the archival process. The organizing thread should be the project itself.

These guidelines are provided so future materials can be processed and included in the collection in a systematic fashion. Staff may also use this procedure for materials already in their position in preparation for the materials being accessioned or registered by the archivist under the park museum collection accountability system, the National Park Service Automated National Cataloging System (ANCS+). Accessioning is the preliminary step in identifying collections that will later be cataloged and processed into the archives. Eventually, finding aids are created to enable staff and researchers to easily access information in the collection archives.

Staff cooperation in carrying out this SOP will greatly accelerate the rate at which materials are processed. Subject matter specialists involved in the creations of these materials carry the greater knowledge about these collections. The quality of the final product will depend upon the quality of staff involvement in the process of identifying the exact nature of archival materials.

Checklist for Preparing Field Documentation:

1) Label all files and describe photographic materials. Fill out one copy of the attached Museum Collection Transfer - Project Identification Sheet for each project or set of records. Also, attach a simple inventory list of formats, i.e. 10 folders, 3 maps, 3 boxes of slides, 2 field notebooks, 2 reports, 1 CD-ROM.

2) Materials must be arranged by material types, such as field notes, report, maps, correspondence, photographs, etc. Each group of materials should be stored in individual folders or acceptable archival enclosures. Remove any personal materials in the files.

3) Resource management staff is responsible for turning over all project documentation to the archivist upon completion of a project. In the interest of preserving institutional knowledge, leave collections in their original order. Original order means the organization system created by the originator of a document collection. Resist the urge to take important documents from these collections. If you need something for future use, copy it or request that the curator make a copy. After copying, replace the

document or photo where you found it. Much information about past projects has been lost because collections have been picked apart. Remember these materials will always be available. That is the intent behind establishing archives.

4) When the archival documentation is transferred to the archivist, the form below would be provided. This form includes the project title, principal investigator, date of project, and a history of the project. The name of the individual who obtained the accession number should also be listed. The type and quantity of documentation would be included as well, such as maps (13), field notes (4 notebooks), correspondence (three files), and so on.

Use one copy of the following Project Identification Sheet for each project or group of records.

[National Park Name]

Museum Collection Transfer - Project Identification **Sheet**

Accession Number_____ (Assigned *Only* By Park Archivist)

Your name _____

Project Title _____

- Principal Investigator and position at the park during project. Please list staff that might have aided project implementation.

_____

- Associated researcher's name, contact information, occupation, employer

_____

- Type and quantity of materials in collection(s) (specimens, paper, files, reports, data, maps, photo prints/negatives/slides, computer media – format/software) Condition. (i.e., infested, torn, broken, good) Attach additional paper if necessary.

_____

- Scope of Project:

Project Title _____

Was a collecting permit issued? No___ Yes ___   Permit Number _____

Were specimens collected? No____ Yes___ Number of specimens_____
If yes, where are they located? _____

List the associated NPS or field catalog numbers (use separate sheet)

Research goals or project purpose, published or in-house reports to which collection relates

_____
_____
_____

Abstract of collection content. Describe the key content of the collection. Refer to geographical locations, processes, data types, associated projects. Attach additional paper if necessary.

Appendix B —
Managing Electronic Mail

On the Record with the Department of the Interior Records Management Program

Electronic Mail... Records...Non-Records...Preserve...Destroy... What do you do?

All employees (and contractors) are required by law to make and preserve records containing adequate and proper documentation of the organization, functions, policies, decisions, procedures, and essential transactions of the agency. In addition, the records must be properly stored and preserved, available for retrieval, and subject to appropriate approved disposition schedules.

The Federal Records Act applies to e-mail records just as it does to records that are created using other media. If you create or receive e-mail messages during the course of your daily work, you are responsible for ensuring that you properly manage them.

The Department's current e-mail policy requires that all e-mails or attachments that meet the definition of a Federal record be added to the organization's files by printing them (including the essential transmission data) and filing them with related paper records.

Remember—electronic mail is intended for official and authorized purposes. You must exercise common sense, good judgment, and propriety when using this government resource. E-mail messages are not private and can be used in court as evidence.

What is an e-mail message?

An e-mail message consists of any document created, transmitted, or received on an e-mail system, including message text and any attachments, such as word-processed documents, spread-sheets, and graphics that may be transmitted with a message, or with an envelope containing no message.

When are e-mail documents records?

E-mail documents are records when they:

- Are created or received in the transaction of agency business;
- Are appropriate for preservation as evidence of the government's function and activities; or
- Are valuable because of the information they contain.

When are e-mail documents not records?

E-mail documents are non-records when they:

- Provide no evidence of agency functions and activities;
- Lack information of value;
- Duplicate information already documented in existing records.

What are my responsibilities?

You are responsible for properly managing the creation, retention, and disposition of records that you send or receive on an e-mail system. You must:

- Determine whether a message—and any attachments—is a record or a non-record as soon as possible after you receive or send it.
- Print a hard copy of the record, including attachments and transmission information, and file it in the official filing system.
- Delete the e-mail version of the record unless you need it for reference purpose.
- Delete messages or attachments that are not records as soon as they have served their purpose.

What about non-records…What do I do with them?

You should promptly delete non-record messages. If non-record copies are useful for reference or convenience, you should copy the information to the hard drive of your computer or to a diskette. Examples of non-records include:

- Copies of memoranda or text sent for information rather than action.

- Instruction memoranda or information bulletins where the recipient is not the action office.

- Messages that have only temporary value such as a message that a meeting time has changed.

If I file my message in a folder I've created in my e-mail system, do I still have to print it and file it in the office's filing system?

Yes. E-mail folders are part of the e-mail system and cannot be part of an official filing system because the e-mail system is protected by use of an individual password accessible only to you. Remember, records must be available for retrieval and access by those who need them.

What about copies of my documents on my laptop computer…Are they records?

All documents (e-mail, word processing, spreadsheets, etc.) on a laptop that meet the definition of a record are considered to be separate documents from similar documents maintained on the computer in your office until they are synchronized and identical.

What happens to the status of my e-mail message after I print it and file it in the office's filing system?

A message that is a record becomes a non-record after the hard copy has been printed and properly retained.

May I use e-mail on my government computer to send personal messages?

Employees on non-duty time are allowed to use Government e-mail systems and computers for limited personal use with the following restrictions. For more detailed guidance refer to AS-PMB Memorandum, June 14, 2000, "Policies on Limited Use of Government Equipment and Telephone Use."

The costs to the Government for the personal use of e-mail must be negligible. Personal use of e-mail must not cause congestion, delay or disruption of service to any Government system or equipment; e.g., by transmitting large attachments.

- Employees may use e-mail for point-to-point electronic transmissions or personal transmissions not to exceed 5 addressees per e-mail both as employee-generated personal messages and in response to personal messages received. Broadcast transmissions, mass mailings or bulletin boards for personal use are prohibited unless specifically authorized by the Bureau or Office System Administrator.

- Employees using e-mail for personal purposes must not represent themselves as acting in an official capacity.

- Employees are reminded to use caution when giving out their Government e-mail address for personal purposes, particularly when "registering" at various Internet sites. Registering may result in the employee receiving unwanted e-mail which in turn could strain the network resources with increased e-mail traffic.

Anything else I need to know?

Yes, very frequently e-mail records are involved in a discovery process during litigation, and/or the subject of congressional requests and Freedom of Information Act (FOIA) requests. If you have e-mail records that are involved in active cases as just described, those records must be preserved. The medium (electronic or paper copy) for preserving e-mail records depends on various factors. In such instances, specific guidance regarding the preservation of relevant records is generally provided either by the Office of Congressional Affairs, the FOIA Officer, or the Office of the Solicitor.

An e-mail message is a record if:

- It contains unique, valuable information developed in preparing position papers, reports, studies, and so on.

- It reflects significant actions taken in the course of conducting business.

- It conveys unique, valuable information about government programs, policies, decisions, or essential actions.

- It conveys statements of policy or the rationale for decisions or actions. It documents oral exchanges (in person or by telephone) during which policy is formulated or other government activities are planned or transacted.

- It adds to the proper understanding of the formulation or execution of government actions or of government operations and responsibilities.

- It documents important meetings or facilitates action by government officials and their successors in office.

- It makes possible a proper scrutiny by the Congress or other duly authorized agencies of the Government.

- It protects the financial, legal, and other rights of the Government and of the persons directly affected by the Government's actions.

Manage your e-mail

- Determine if the e-mail message/attachments meet the legal definition of a record.

- Print a hard copy of the record, including attachments and transmission information, and file it in the official filing system.

- Delete the e-mail version of the record unless you need it for reference purposes.

- Delete messages or attachments that are not records as soon as they have served their purpose.

- Always treat a message as a record first if you are unsure about its correct status.

Appendix C —
Recommended Procedures for Submitting Cataloging Requests to the PWR Regional Library

Please follow these procedures, when submitting title pages for cataloging by the Pacific West Regional Library in Seattle. This will help provide fast and efficient service.

- Photocopy the title page and the page with the copyright information (this is usually the page behind the title page). For government publications and reports this information may be on the cover or last page of the publication.

- Mark or stamp the photocopies with the park name. Note the park library sub-collection if applicable and the copy number if this book is in addition to a copy already in the collection or if you want multiple copies cataloged.

- Send the photocopies to the Pacific West Regional Library at 168 South Jackson Street, Seattle, WA 98104: Attention Cataloging.

The catalog records created by the Regional Library are uploaded into Voyager, the online combined catalog of NPS Libraries. This catalog is available through the Internet at **www.library.nps.gov**. Limits can be used to restrict searches to just the resources of your park. A local catalog of just your park's material can be sent to you from the Regional Library. This can be setup on a computer in the library or printouts can be made. This local catalog should be updated frequently by contacting the Regional Library for a new copy.

Catalog labels will be sent back as soon as possible. In a few cases, it might be necessary to send in the book if original cataloging is necessary. When the label set is received, follow park procedures for processing the book. Here are some basic procedures if the park does not have specific instructions:

- Find the book on the "new books shelf" or in the book processing area.

- Glue in a book pocket, generally on the inside cover, either in the front or the back. Try not to obscure any unique maps or illustrations.

- Each label set has two horizontal rectangular stickers (7.5cm x 2.5cm). Place one on the top of the book-pocket and the other on the top of the checkout card.

- Next, there will be a smaller rectangular sticker (2.3cm x 2.8cm) with your parks acronym such as "HAFO," "LARO-KF," "MORA-SUN" or "FOCL-RARE" on it. Place this label on the pouch part of the pocket to help identify the park and collection that the book belongs to. Some park libraries do not use this label. However, all books need to be stamped or otherwise marked to indicate ownership by your park library.

- Finally, on the upper left-hand corner of the label set, there will be a sticker (2.3cm x 3.8cm) on which is printed a call number. Place this call number sticker on the bottom of the spine if it is possible to see the whole call number. If the spine is too narrow then put this sticker on the bottom left-hand corner of the cover page. Cover this sticker with a clear plastic label or tape to prevent the label from getting worn and illegible.

- If the book in question has a book jacket, a protective plastic cover may be put on it after affixing labels. These plastic covers are available from library supply vendors. They exist in a variety of sizes, so take the one closest in size to the book jacket with which you are working.

To shelve the books:

- 1. The books are ordered first alphabetically by letter (A before E, QA before QE); then by number (482.345 before 482.4); then by a letter-number combination; finally by year (if provided). Occasionally, there will be additional information provided (copy number; "draft"), which should also be arranged alpha-numerically.

- 2. Determine what call number the book in question has, then find where on the shelf it should be placed. Shift surrounding materials as necessary. If it is labeled as belonging to a special collection, shelve it accordingly.

Contact:
Nancy Hori, Lead Librarian
Pacific West Regional Library, National Park Service
168 South Jackson Street
Seattle, WA 98104
(206) 220-4154 / (206) 652-1431 fax
nancy_hori@nps.gov

NPS Online Information Resources

Resource	Description	Site address
RECORDS MANAGEMENT	Guidance for NPS records management can be located on the web, including the NPS Records Handbook, *DO #19* Records Retention Schedule and other helpful instructions and links. Contact: Susan Ewing Haley, PW Regional Records Manager 415-561-4804 (phone at GOGA) susan_ewing_haley@nps.gov **See also doilearn for online records management course**	General information **inside.nps.gov/records management/ guidance and instruction** *DO #19* Records Retention Schedule: **Inside.nps.gov/records management/guidance and instruction/records management schedule.pdf**
NPS FOCUS DIGITAL LIBRARY & RESEARCH STATION	NPS FOCUS is a service supported digital library that searches across many databases and data sets in a single search, creating a one-stop-shopping site for electronic information. You can choose from a list of NPS and other outside resources to search. Full text documents, reports, plans and articles are available, as are images, maps, drawings and web pages. Images can be viewed and downloaded in many sizes through the built-in DejaVu image viewing tool. You can link images or reports to PMIS projects if you post them on FOCUS. Contact: NPS_Focus@nps.gov	TO SEARCH: NPS intranet site: **http://focus.inside.nps.gov/** public site: **http://npsfocus.nps.gov/** TO ENTER DATA: To post items take online course from doilearn (http://www.doiu.nbc.gov/) then fax completion certificate to FOCUS data manager to acquire a password.
NPS LIBRARY	One system for searching across thousands of library catalogs, the current tables of contents for 12,000 journals, plus citations (with abstracts) for current journal literature, conference proceedings, studies, and dissertations covering multiple disciplines. Do your own searches or use the NPS Ask-a-Librarian service to request assistance. Can also be searched through FOCUS.	Catalogs and links: http://www.library.nps.gov/ Contacts: Nancy Hori – PWR Librarian, Seattle RO Amalin Ferguson –NPS Library Program Manager
DOI ELECTRONIC RESOURCES	U.S. Department of the Interior employees may use ten database services to discover and obtain congressional, executive, and judicial documents, and articles from a wide spectrum of journals, conference proceedings, magazines, newsletters, and newspapers.	**http://library.doi.gov/databases.html**

Name	Description	URL / Contact
NATUREBIB	NPS bibliographic and full text articles of published natural and cultural resources literature, gray literature, park reports, plans and documents.	**Public site:** http://www.nature.nps.gov/nrbib/ **Data entry:** **https://science1.nature.nps.gov/naturebib/nb/simple/clean** Apply for a password through Network I & M data manager
NPS PACIFIC ISLANDS CORAL REEF PROGRAM	Preserving, and where necessary restoring, native isolated coral reef ecosystems the National Park Service entered into a Cooperative Study Agreement with the University of Hawaii--the forerunner of this present CESU. This Cooperative Science endeavor has developed science and strategies which today form the basis for managing to preserve native island ecosystems. Among the study products are more than a hundred technical reports funded by the NPS and others.	**http://www.botany.hawaii.edu/basch/uhnpscesu/picrp/** **home.htm** Contact: Dr. Larry Basch, specialist in marine invertebrates, National Park Service Scientist at the University of Hawaii Cooperative Ecosystem Unit (CESU UH).
NPS NATIONAL MUSEUM CATALOG	NPS collections span many themes, time-periods, geographic areas, individuals, groups, cultures, movements, ecosystems and disciplines. Located at more than 300 parks throughout the country, the collections represent the disciplines of archeology; ethnology; history (including art and archives); biology; paleontology and geology. Artifact and specimen catalog records, many include photos.	**http://www.museum.nps.gov/**
NPS MUSEUM PROGRAM PUBLICATIONS	*Museum Handbook, Conserv-O-Grams*, ANCS+ User Manual, Curatorial Safety Messages, Disaster Planning, bibliography	**http://www.nps.gov/history/museum/publications/** **index.htm**
NPS HISTORY AND CULTURE WEB PORTAL	Portal to NPS History and Culture website includes links to databases: HABS/HAER, National Register of Historic Places, NPS Historic Photograph Collection at Harpers Ferry Center, Contact list to cultural programs, online publications including *Common Ground*, *CRM Journal*, *Heritage News* and others.	**http://www.nps.gov/history/collections.htm**

PARK HISTORIES	A collection of full text park histories and NPS history. Some copyright restrictions.	http://www.nps.gov/history/history/history/park histories/ index htm
MAPS AND GIS DATA **USGS FGDC**	NOAA National Geophysical Data Center (NGDC) NDEP is for producers and users of elevation data NOAA National Ocean Service (NOS) Data Explorer USACE National Coastal Data Bank (NCDB) + more databases	**http://www.geodata.gov**

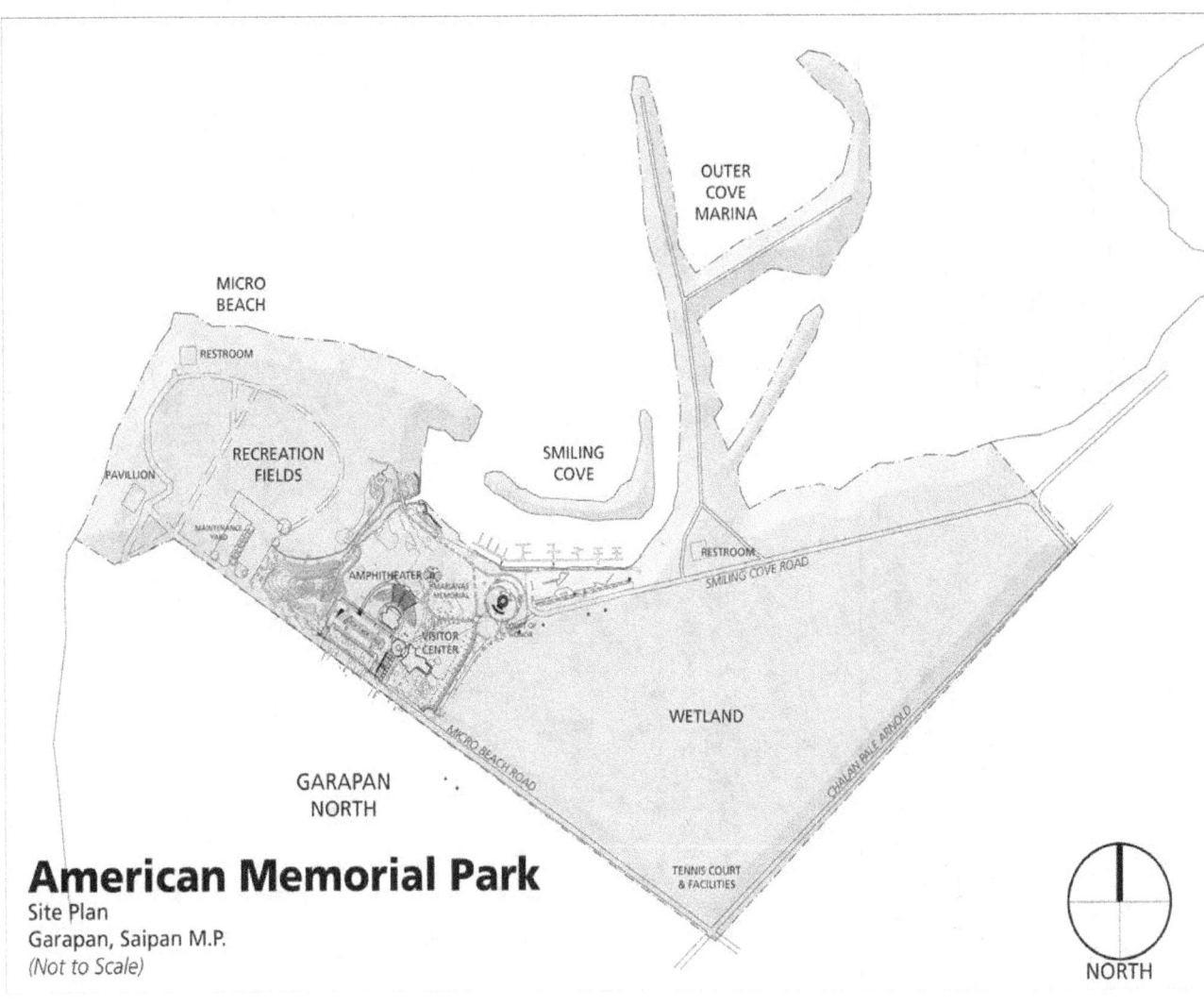

MICRO
BEACH

RESTROOM

PAVILLION

RECREATION
FIELDS

MAINTENANCE
YARD

AMPHITHEATER

MARIANAS
MEMORIAL

VISITOR
CENTER

OUTER
COVE
MARINA

SMILING
COVE

RESTROOM

SMILING COVE ROAD

WETLAND

MICRO BEACH ROAD

CHALAN PALE ARNOLD

GARAPAN
NORTH

TENNIS COURT
& FACILITIES

American Memorial Park

Site Plan
Garapan, Saipan M.P.
(Not to Scale)

NORTH

www.ingramcontent.com/pod-product-compliance
Lightning Source LLC
Chambersburg PA
CBHW081504170526
45166CB00008B/2552